Spirit H

Spirit Healing

by Bob Woodward

Floris Books

First published in 2004 by Floris Books
© 2004 Bob Woodward

The moral right of the author has been asserted

All rights reserved. No part of this publication may
be reproduced without the prior permission of
Floris Books, 15 Harrison Gardens, Edinburgh.

British Library CIP Data available

ISBN 086315-444-1

Printed in Great Britain
by The Bath Press, Bath

Dedicated to Ray and Joan Branch
with gratitude

Contents

Foreword

Spiritual healing. What associations do these words have for us? Perhaps: gentle, non-confrontational, subtle, mysterious. Among scientifically minded people or 'non-believers' there might be scepticism or frank ridicule.

We live in an age when, on one hand, everything we do has to have justifiable method and statistically-proven efficacy. On the other, ill or suffering people are seeking help from a bewildering array of alternative or complementary approaches. We can consider these in the light of the 'will to heal' — and the 'will to be healed.' Are we seeking to be free of illness, comfortable again, or for healing in the sense of becoming whole? Spiritual healing is at the heart of these questions and is not, in spite of first impressions, simply passive or unconscious for the recipient. In modern parlance we could describe it as having minimum method and maximum 'attitude'!

I heard Harry Edwards speak at a health and healing conference some thirty years ago. He stood out as a man of quiet, solid integrity at a time when sensational, charismatic methods caught the limelight. I received one healing session with Bob, a self-reflective experience which gave benefit, also in unexpected ways. In this book Bob brings helpful light to bear on spiritual healing, which we can see as a subtle but active manifestation of Christ's saying: 'For where two or three are gathered together in my name, there I am in the midst of them.'

Dr Hugh Gayer
The Sheiling School Medical Officer

The Author

Bob Woodward has been active within the healing profession of Curative Education for some thirty years, living with and educating children and young people with Special Educational Needs. Throughout that time he has lived and worked within Camphill, a movement now comprising nearly one hundred communities world-wide and which, since its inception in 1940, continues to have very clear therapeutic and healing tasks, particularly in the field of social and community-building endeavours.[1] The underlying philosophy of both Curative Education and Camphill is based on Rudolf Steiner's anthroposophy — a holistic worldview which takes account of the spiritual realities and relationships in the human being and the cosmos.

He received his secondary education for some seven years at Wynstones School, a Rudolf Steiner School in Gloucestershire and, in later life, became a graduate of the University of Bristol where he was awarded two Masters degrees.

Bob Woodward has been a student of anthroposophy for nearly forty years, and has been very interested in spiritual healing for at least twenty-five years. He is a full-healer member of the Bristol District Association of Healers and also of the World Federation of Healing. He is married, has three sons and two daughters, and lives with his wife and family at the Sheiling School Camphill Community in Thornbury, near Bristol. Over the past two years, and with the written request and consent of pupils' parents, he has been able to offer individual sessions of spiritual healing to some children and youngsters with special needs.

Bob Woodward has a special interest in childhood autism and is co-author of the book, *Autism — A Holistic Approach* published by Floris Books.

Acknowledgments

I am very grateful to the following people who gave their time to read an earlier draft of this book and provided me with constructive comments and also frank criticisms which I have duly taken heed of in thoroughly reworking the manuscript now one year hence.

Ray Branch — formerly of the Harry Edwards Spiritual Healing Sanctuary at Burrows Lea in Surrey. Together with his wife, Joan, Ray Branch worked very closely with Harry Edwards himself and, following the latter's death in 1976, they continued to serve the healing work of 'The Sanctuary' at Burrows Lea for more than 25 years until their recent retirement. He is the author of a fascinating biography of Harry Edwards.

Dr Jean Brown — a very experienced anthroposophical medical doctor, and a personal friend, who made many invaluable suggestions and raised important questions from the anthroposophical perspective.

Dr Jack Angelo — a well-known and respected writer and teacher in the field of subtle energy medicine and natural spirituality. He is also a trainer for the National Federation of Spiritual Healers.

Dennis and Doreen Fare — healers of long-standing and high repute who had the challenging task of introducing me into the practice of hands on spiritual healing. Dennis Fare is a former President of the National Federation of Spiritual Healers and of the World Federation of Healing.

Hazel Townsley — who, once again, took on the unenviable task of converting my manuscripts into clear and publishable print.

Introduction

There are already many good books available on the theme of spiritual healing written by healers with many years of experience to draw on.

My reason in writing this small volume is not to repeat what can be better read, and in detail, elsewhere, but rather to try to throw some further and perhaps a new light on spiritual healing in the light of Rudolf Steiner's comprehensive *Anthroposophy*. This is something which, to my knowledge, has not been previously attempted and I would therefore like this work to be regarded more as a research thesis than as any finished and final project.

Whereas some healers are also clairvoyant to a degree,[1] and able to perceive what is taking place on higher levels of reality than the physically sense-perceptible, Rudolf Steiner (1861–1925), in addition to having natural clairvoyance as a child, also became an Initiate of the highest standing. Initiation-knowledge means that not only are the spiritual sense organs (chakras) opened and perceiving on the levels of Soul and Spirit, but that the one who is thus able to perceive also clearly understands what it is he or she sees. Just as on the physical level, knowledge is more than the mere ability to receive impressions and percepts, so in the higher worlds a true understanding and knowing requires much more than the faculty of clairvoyance alone. Steiner's thirty or so written books and his 6000 printed lectures bear testament to the incredible breadth and depth of his spiritual understanding and knowledge. He was above all a research scientist,[2] who however did not confine his investigations to the level of the sense-bound intellect.

Particularly in the last seven years of his life, the results of

Steiner's initiate-knowledge, or spiritual science, began to be implemented in many very practical areas of life.[3] Included in this was an extension of the Art of Healing brought about through courses of lectures given to medical doctors and students. From its inception modern anthroposophical medicine[4] was seen as complementary to ordinary medicine rather than as an alternative. While it was clearly Steiner's task, in meeting the requests which came towards him, to give clear guidelines for a 'rational medical therapy' based on an intimate knowledge of the human being in relation to the kingdoms of nature, there are also a number of important indications by him of the reality of psychic and spiritual healing. A main task of this book is therefore to make those indications which he gave more widely known, whilst also drawing on various other aspects of anthroposophical spiritual science to illuminate this increasingly popular and acknowledged form of complementary therapy. Already in 1954, Canon Shepherd in his book on the life and work of Rudolf Steiner commented that:

> During Steiner's lifetime spirit-healing was hardly recognised, but at the present time it is being looked upon with much more favour, both by the Christian Churches and by the medical profession, and is spreading widely.[5]

Ultimately I hope that an informed and fruitful collaboration will come about between doctors, whether practising allopathic, homeopathic, or anthroposophical medicine, and qualified spiritual healers, in order to offer the very best treatment and support to those who are sick and suffering. In order to do this a truly holistic recognition of the human being in body, soul, and spirit needs to supersede the current genetic and biochemical model which so strongly dominates the Western mainstream medical profession. This model also underpins the widespread popularization of the many new advances and breakthroughs in medical research and technology. However these advances are based not on a holistic knowledge of human nature but rather on the reductionist materialistic science that has increasingly influenced all aspects of modern life since its beginnings in the fifteenth and sixteenth centuries. That this narrow viewpoint, for all its stunning achievements, is actually inadequate to promote genuine human health and healing is, I believe, becoming increasingly apparent to many thinking people. Already eighty years ago, in 1924, in a course of lectures which Rudolf Steiner gave to doctors and priests he felt called upon to say that:

> To be a healer requires first and foremost a spiritual outlook on the world. And indeed the greatest anomaly of our time is this, that it is medicine itself that has the frightful disease: materialism. Medicine is seriously ill with materialism.[6]

Although this book is particularly directed to people who already know at least something of Rudolf Steiner's anthroposophy, but little or nothing about spiritual healing, I also hope that healers who wish to gain a clearer understanding of their own practices will find an anthroposophical viewpoint as presented here both informative and enlightening. Finally, perhaps members of the public who have already experienced some of the benefits of spiritual healing, as well as those who may have recourse to it in the future, will also find the contents of this book to be of interest.

1. Spiritual Healing — Contact and Distant

Spiritual healing is defined by the self-regulatory body for spiritual healing practitioners in the United Kingdom as:

> The channelling of healing energy through the hands and/or with thought. It does not include massage, manipulation, the use of instruments, drugs or other remedies or the practice of clairvoyance or psychic surgery. It does include Distant or Absent Healing.[8]

Our hands are uniquely human. I remember reading once that not even the most highly developed apes have a comparable formation of their hands to those of human beings.

With our hands we are enabled to do a great variety of things, not least of which is to express caring, concern, and affection for others. With our hands we can also give help and healing; whether it be to lead a child by the hand or perhaps to rub a bruised knee better!

Before and during the time of Christ the laying-on-of-hands for the purposes of healing has been practised. Practised by Christ himself and his disciples, and practised by innumerable healers up to our present time.

It can be sensed that in the palm of each hand there is a minor chakra, or energy centre, through which healing energies can flow once the chakra is active and open. Since one hand, the right, is principally for giving and the other, the left, is principally for receiving, the two hands working together in healing both complement and support each other.

In different books on healing we can read of a variety of techniques or methods for the laying-on-of-hands. Often these will involve touching over the seven main chakra sites, located from the crown of the head to the base of the spine (for a full description see the table on page 95). Experienced healers make it clear that what they describe in their books is what they have found to work best for them and their patients, and that their techniques may therefore serve as useful guidelines for others developing on the healing path. Therefore each healer must gradually discover his or her own way and take on board, so to speak, from others, what feels right for them.

However the outer practices and methods may vary, what can safely be said to be invariable and common to all healers whatever their level of experience, are the basic attitudes of sympathy, compassion, and service, towards those who are sick and suffering. There is a fundamental will-to-heal, to extend help and support in any and every way that is within the healer's power to perform.

While the power of spiritual healing may well be looked upon as a gift of God, or of the Divine, it is likely that it is also an inherent human potential which can be developed further through practice and perseverance, provided that the basic attitudes of sympathy, compassion, and willingness to offer help, are genuinely present in heart and mind. This was eloquently expressed by Harry Edwards in the foreword to his comprehensive and landmark book, *A Guide to the Understanding and Practice of Spiritual Healing*, when he writes:

> The following question is often asked by people who wish they possessed the gift of healing, 'Do you think I could become a healer?' and when I speak to gatherings on the subject of spiritual healing, I often ask the

> audience, 'How many of you would like to be the means of healing reaching the sick?' Usually a high percentage will raise their hands.
>
> The answer [to the first quotation] is, 'People who have a deep inner yearning to give of themselves in healing the sick, to take away pain and stress, who possess compassion and sympathy for those who are afflicted and are willing to sacrifice their time without any pecuniary reward; people who are generous in their nature, and who render willing service for good causes, are those who possess the spiritual qualities which mark the healing gift.
>
> This healing potential, then, only needs the development of the faculty of attunement with the spirit source of healing and the opportunity to give it practical expression.[9]

One essential quality that needs to be developed, and which can only be gained through doing, is 'faith' in *the healing power itself*, or, to use a word that does not have obvious religious connotations, 'confidence.' In the two years of practice as a probationer healer (which is common to healing organizations in the UK), the opportunity is provided to strengthen one's confidence and certainty in the help that is given from the spiritual world. Indeed spiritual healing is nothing without the conviction that there are indeed real spiritual sources, wellsprings, from which healing forces or energies can, and do, flow. In this respect some of the literature refers to a 'universal energy field.' Most healers view and experience themselves as being conscious instruments, or channels, through which healing energies can flow to those in need. As the world renowned healer, Harry Edwards, pointed out, he himself had never healed anyone! Rather the healing energies, working through him, had brought about the good results seen in many thousands of people.

Edwards, who died in 1976, was convinced that the healing energies or forces were directed by spirit guides and helpers working from the other side of life into earthly existence. This viewpoint appears to be commonly held by many modern healers irrespective of whether the healer's actual role in this co-operative working is seen as relatively simple,[10] or as much more complex and scientific.[11]

A spiritual healer is not a doctor, though some doctors are also spiritual healers, and therefore does not have the medical knowledge to make diagnoses or to prescribe treatments. But many healers believe that their guides and helpers in Spirit do have advanced knowledge and insights and are thereby able to direct specific energies, together with the necessary intensity, towards an individual patient's health needs. In this scenario the fundamental task of the healer is to be as good, as pure a channel or instrument as possible, so that the healing forces can be of maximum effectiveness and benefit. One can here be reminded of the aspiration expressed in the first words of the beautiful prayer of St Francis of Assisi, himself an outstanding healer in the early thirteenth century,

Lord, make me an instrument of your peace.

In the light of what has been said so far, the question could of course be raised: Is it appropriate nowadays, given our modern independent thinking consciousness, for a person to try to train themselves as an instrument or channel for spiritual forces, and/or beings, to work through? Is this perhaps a throwback to a more atavistic, instinctive state of consciousness and, therefore, even unhealthy in our time? This question will particularly be raised by those who are already familiar with the teachings of Rudolf Steiner since his spiritual science, or anthroposophy, lays great stress on the need for wide-awake and independent thinking consciousness. Any lowering of normal consciousness in spiritual development, in the sense of sinking into a trance or dream-like state, was considered by Steiner as completely inappropriate for modern times. As a life-long student of anthroposophy I wholeheartedly agree that a free, independent and awake thinking consciousness is certainly a necessity and a safeguard. However, as a healer, I also know through direct experience, that modern spiritual healing can be done without in any way sacrificing one's awake consciousness, inner freedom, and self-control. Indeed the conscious healing act, or service, actually leads to a heightened experience of spiritual attunement and ethical responsibility. An inner peace and a certain freedom from one's everyday worries, concerns, and personal hang-ups, is essential in order to come into the *state of attunement* prior to and during healing.

Significantly, Harry Edwards maintained that the practice and experience of spiritual healing has, in reality, a much bigger purpose, namely, to help awaken an awareness both for our own spiritual nature as well as for the spiritual, or divine, in the cosmos. This same purpose may also be said of Rudolf Steiner's anthroposophy.

To summarize what has been described so far in this chapter we can say that in hands-on (or contact) spiritual healing:

The hands are used to convey healing energies or forces;
The healer's attitude, based on sympathy, compassion, and the will-to-heal, is of fundamental importance;
A healer strives to become a *conscious* channel, or instrument, for spiritual healing energies; and,
Many healers believe that they are working in co-operation

with guides and helpers from across the Threshold, i.e. discarnate human souls and/or spiritual beings, such as healing angels.

Spiritual healing is however not limited or restricted in its application by either space or time. Whilst direct hands-on contact healing may be the form in which spiritual healing is most often pictured, it is likely that the use of 'absent' or better said 'distant' healing is in fact the more widely practised of these two methods. Certainly this is very much the case in the healing work that is conducted at the Harry Edwards Spiritual Healing Sanctuary in Surrey, England, where thousands of requests for absent healing are still received each week from all over the world. Edwards himself believed that absent healing because of its access and availability, independent of geographical location and fixed times, was a much more advanced method of spiritual healing than that given through direct contact.

> It can be truly said that Absent Healing will become the most potent healing factor for the future. If one accepts the truth that patients suffering from medically incurable conditions can be cured solely through Absent Healing we establish the foundation for a healing revelation of the greatest magnitude.[12]

(Not, of course, that Edwards here claims that all patients with incurable conditions will be healed through absent healing.)

Whilst Harry Edwards was undoubtedly a pioneer in the whole field of spiritual healing and particularly so in his advocacy and practice of absent healing, it is clear from the literature that healing at a distance has become a method that many spiritual healers have also adopted. Just as with contact healing there are a wide variety of methods and techniques (perhaps possibly as many as there are healers), with absent healing also various practices are used. However, in all cases, the essentials remain common to all forms of spiritual healing. Namely there must be a link up, by means of a request for healing between the healer and the patient and, similarly, a link via attunement between the healer and the spiritual source(s) of healing energies or forces. It is therefore particularly clear that with absent or distant healing the role of the healer is simply that of an intermediary or instrument within the healing process. Indeed, it is quite conceivable that if any person becomes aware and awake to the reality of turning consciously to the spiritual world, with a request for their own healing needs, recourse to a particular spiritual healer might prove to be unnecessary! As we have already noted, Harry Edwards was convinced that the greater purpose behind the reality of spiritual healing was none other than to awaken people to the Spirit and, thereby, to overcome any narrow materialistic worldview.

It is especially in regard to healing at a distance that Edwards' notion of spirit doctors (guides and helpers), comes to the foreground when seeking a viable explanation of how this method is altogether possible. With contact healing the actual physical presence of both healer and patient, the reassurance and comfort which hands-on touch conveys, the verbal interchange and signs of compassionate understanding and support from the healer, all contribute to the healing ethos and experience. However in the case of absent healing this form of intimate directness is removed, and yet many years of practice bear clear testimony to the effectiveness of this method.[13] The published evidence provides additional credence to the notion of direct intercession and assistance following a patient's request for help, via the healer, given from purely spiritual sources. In the words of Harry Edwards,

> That consequent upon the emission of a thought appeal by a human mind in attunement with a spirit intelligence, the spirit guide is able to receive the request and to administer the correct quality of force to heal the particular disharmony in the body of the patient.[14]

That thoughts are indeed psychic realities was emphasized by Rudolf Steiner. A good, kind, or compassionate thought directed to someone, wherever they may be geographically, will have a positive, healthy effect upon them. The converse is also true if thoughts of dislike, revenge, hatred, etc. are sent from one person towards another. In spiritual healing, and perhaps particularly so in the case of absent healing, a clear thought intentionality and thought directive is required. This gives a definite focus and strength to the healing request, which is mentally sent to the spirit guides and helpers. It is therefore also common practice in absent healing to ask for regular, though brief, written or verbal updates to be given to the healer by the patient or by the one who is requesting healing on his or her behalf. This regular communication, acknowledged and replied to by the healer, is an important means of maintaining the human and spiritual link-up and of ensuring that the spirit guides have up-to-date information on the state of the patient. Based on this information the required healing energies are then made available.

However, whether, for example, a physical healing inevitably takes place is dependent on a number of factors. From the anthroposophical viewpoint, karmic and individual circumstances and possibilities will be of major significance. Spiritual healing is governed by laws of life, and is neither arbitrary nor random. Healing does not always result in a cure but, on the other hand, when healing has been requested the call will never go unanswered and appropriate help will be offered in one way or another. Whether the patient is sufficiently ready and receptive to receive this help, particularly if it does not manifest in the form hoped for, is of course also a major factor in the process of healing. True healing can only take place when the laws of life and karma permit, and depends not only on the healer's will to do everything possible to help, but also upon the patient's own will and determination to be healed. Indeed it could well be argued that, ultimately, all genuine healing (and not just a temporary masking of symptoms) really amounts to *'self-healing*.' Doctors, surgeons, therapists, and healers, can all play a vital part in this process but without the will of the patient to get well, or perhaps in the case of a sick child the relative's will, a successful healing outcome is hardly possible. This active will, with the expectation and anticipation of an improvement in health, probably goes a long way towards explaining the well-known placebo effect, whereby a patient can show marked improvement because he believes he has received some particular form of treatment but, in fact, has not! This phenomenon of, we could say, 'mind over matter,' may have a very positive part to play in the efficacy of some spiritual healings. However, healing can also be effective when the patient has no knowledge that help has been sought on his or her behalf. Therefore spiritual healing is not synonymous with so-called 'faith healing,' in which the patient's belief or faith in the healing act or process is regarded as vital.

> It is not necessary for the patient to believe or even to know anything about the healing, although it is best if he himself asks for help and, if he can tune in consciously knowing what hour the healing is going to be given, this too is beneficial. In any case the amount of

> healing he can absorb will only be that which his higher self desires, that which is right for him. With absent healing, just as with contact healing, we should take the patient closer to his higher self ...[15]

Spiritual healing is holistic and must reckon with body, soul, and spirit. Therefore the efficacy of both contact and distant healing to help overcome illness and disease, sometimes when all else has failed, may well serve to convince many that there is more to us than only physical matter and genes!

2. Steiner's Anthroposophy

Since the specific intention of this book is to examine spiritual healing in the light of Rudolf Steiner's anthroposophy, or spiritual science, and since his teachings may still today be largely unknown to many people, I will describe, albeit briefly in this chapter some of the basic tenets of Steiner's holistic worldview.

The most comprehensive account of this worldview is to be found in one of Steiner's fundamental books, first published in 1909 and revised by him in 1925, and most recently reprinted in 1997 with the title, *An Outline of Esoteric Science*. However in addition to his actual writings, Steiner also gave very many lectures, most of which have since been translated into English from the original German (Steiner was by birth Austrian), but which, with very few exceptions, were not checked or corrected by him from the shorthand reports which were made whilst he lectured. Two of these early lecture courses, given in the years 1906 and 1907 respectively (see Bibliography), also give a very helpful wide-ranging account of the whole field of spiritual science, dealing not only with the differentiated nature of the human being but also with the various stages in the course of world evolution.

According to Steiner's spiritual researches, the human being consists of four distinct members. The outer material body is visible to our ordinary sense perception, but the higher supersensible members of the human being can only be observed with the aid of awakened organs of spiritual perception such as Rudolf Steiner himself possessed. Though Steiner was, I'm sure, not singular in having such powers of supersensible cognition, his spiritual-scientific researches led him to a remarkable depth and breadth of perception and knowledge and this is so obviously apparent through the contents of his extensive published works. Steiner also described in detail how the spiritual organs of perception, latent in all human beings, can be systematically developed through careful and methodical training, which involves the practice of exercises in concentration and meditation.[1] He was however at pains to point out that any one step taken towards the attainment of higher knowledge necessitated three steps taken towards the perfection of one's own character. In other words, for Rudolf Steiner, the inner path of higher development was, at the same time, a moral and ethical path requiring considerable patience, perseverance, and earnestness. It is noteworthy that he himself, though possessing a natural clairvoyance, did not speak openly of his spiritual-scientific researches until the beginning of the twentieth century when he was already forty years of age. Steiner only spoke of spiritual matters after he had first made thorough, rigorous, and methodical investigations following the way of scientific research, which was however not limited to observation of the outer, sense-perceptible, world. His use of particular terminology in respect of the human being's complex holistic constitution was very precise, as can be well seen in *Theosophy*, one of his fundamental books.

Another major consideration for him was the justification and cultural need to speak openly about matters which traditionally had been guarded and kept secret.

In his autobiography Steiner writes:

> Moreover, I was under no obligation to anyone to guard mysteries, for I accepted nothing out of 'ancient wisdom'; what I possess of spiritual knowledge is entirely the result of my own research. Only when an

> item of knowledge has come to me, I then introduce whatever of the 'ancient knowledge' has already been made public from some direction or other, in order to point to the harmony between the two and, at the same time, the advance which is possible to contemporary research.
>
> Thus, after a certain point of time, it was quite clear to me that in the public presentation of spiritual knowledge I should be doing the right thing.[2]

The human being has, says Steiner, in addition to a material body of flesh and blood, also an etheric body, an astral body, and an Ego. He is therefore a fourfold being. Steiner describes how these members are perceived with higher vision but, even without such personal vision, it is very well possible to understand through thinking and through their perceptible effects, the particular nature of each of these normally invisible members. The etheric body, which Steiner also sometimes referred to as the 'life-body' or 'body of formative forces,' is responsible for enlivening and giving form and shape to the earthly material body and all the organ-systems therein. Without it our biological organism would quickly begin to disintegrate, as indeed it does when death occurs. The etheric body therefore remains united with the earthly material body throughout our lives, also during the periods of sleep.

However this is not the case with the astral (or soul) body which each night withdraws itself from the physical and etheric bodies and enters, together with the fourth member of our being, 'the I' or Ego, into worlds of Soul and Spirit. In the morning, on awakening, the astral body and Ego re-enter the two 'lower' members, and we once more regain our normal daily awake ego-consciousness, and set about dealing with the tasks and responsibilities of the new day. The astral body is, says Steiner, the bearer of consciousness, through which we become aware of our life of thoughts, feelings, and will impulses. In other words, the varied 'landscape' of our inner soul-life. However within this soul-life, and for each person, there arises, like the Sun at dawn, the clear consciousness and focus of our very own selfhood, our 'I' nature. It is clear that all of us have a unique biography and destiny and this is due to the fact that we are indeed Egos, each in his or her own right. This constitutes our actual human core, our real spiritual being. Our normal everyday individual I-consciousness, or ego-consciousness, can only be indicative of our true being, rather like a reflection in a mirror. The path of inner development and training, enables us to gradually transcend our limited, mirrored, earthly ego-consciousness, and rise, so to speak, towards our own true spiritual nature. These important differentiations can be shown diagramatically in this way.

The Fourfold Human Being	
Members	**Realm**
Ego	Spirit
Astral Body	Soul
Etheric Body	Life
Physical Body	Mineral

At death, or soon after, the three supersensible members of our being, namely the etheric and astral bodies and the Ego, free themselves from the material remains and begin to live in their own proper realms. In time the etheric body dissolves into the world ether, and the astral body into the astral or soul world, but the Ego on its further journey into purely spiritual realms of being, takes with it the hard won fruits of earthly life as essences or extracts of the individual's etheric and astral bodies.

Eventually there comes a 'moment' in the life of the spirit after death (the so-called cosmic midnight hour) when a new decision is made to prepare for the descent to a further life on earth. In the systematic course of this descent soul and life 'substances' will be provided for the building of new astral and etheric bodies which will, eventually, come to be united with the material body provided by the parents through the forces of heredity and genetic make-up. In reality all this involves complex and intricate processes which are guided and helped by higher spiritual beings. (There are nine ranks, or hierarchies, of more highly developed beings, which include the angels and archangels.)

The teaching of reincarnation and destiny, or karma, is central to Steiner's anthroposophy. This teaching is however not conceived like the inexorable, and fatalistic, 'Wheel of Life' known to Eastern beliefs, such as Buddhism, but it is seen in the light of a progressive Christ-Impulse. A Christ-Impulse which does not at all depend on the variety of religious Christian beliefs, faiths, and dogmas, but which has seen a world-encompassing objective reality ever since the Mystery of Golgotha (i.e. the Passion, Death and Resurrection) and the subsequent uniting of the Christ Being with the whole future evolution of the planet and humankind. Steiner referred to the world significance of the Christ-Impulse in many of his lectures.[3] He also made it very clear that whereas in earlier times the Christ-Impulse worked in human hearts that did not yet grasp with real understanding and consciousness the nature of this Impulse, that time has now past.

> We shall see one thing clearly: the time when Christ worked in the way I have described is past and gone,

> and the time has come when men must *understand* Christ, must have real knowledge of Christ.[4]

What was possible and, so to speak, legitimate in earlier times does not hold good in the same way in later times. Each incarnation, or earthly life, provides us with needed opportunities for personal growth and development as beings of soul and spirit. One life would simply not suffice for that long evolutionary path of learning and development which all of us are on, whether we are consciously aware of it or not.

Therefore, according to anthroposophy, we have lived again and again on earth, in different historical and pre-historical periods and epochs. There will come a time when, as a matter of course, we will be able to remember our last previous incarnation, but for most people at the present time we have no clear recollection of who we once were nor what we did. This knowledge is however known to our own angel (the guardian angel) who accompanies us from life to life, from incarnation to incarnation. It is known also to other higher beings who help us in our life after death to plan for the new life on earth in the light of what we have done, or not done, in the past, and therefore what we will aim to achieve in the coming earthly existence. More and more in our time Christ Himself becomes the new 'Lord of Karma' who is aware of the consequences, for the Earth's evolution, of each person's sins and errors, and brings to meet these His cosmic power of redemption and forgiveness.[5] However Christ's intervention for the sake of humanity's progress, does not in any way excuse us from the effects of karmic justice on the level of the individual. Our deeds in one life are linked, through karmic laws, to our situation and circumstances, our talents and propensities, in the succeeding life and we are thus responsible for shaping our new destiny and karma. We must indeed later reap what we ourselves have sown, wittingly or unwittingly!

When viewed in the light of reincarnation and karma such events as illness and disease, also so-called accidents and misadventures, can look very different than when they are perceived only in the context of a single and isolated lifetime.[6] In effect this means that when such events do occur in the unique biographical tapestry of a person's life on earth, they have meaning and significance. With this we have at least the beginnings of a viable explanation of why one person may recover from a serious life-threatening illness, whilst another person, perhaps receiving comparable medical or other treatments (including perhaps spiritual healing), may succumb. In their insightful book, *The Seven Levels of Healing*, the authors who are also both healers write that:

> ... some people will not get better because it is their Karma to live through the illness and learn from it. If an illness fails to respond either to orthodox treatment or to healing, we can presume that it is Karmic. If there is Karma to be paid, or there are lessons to be learnt, the patient may become calmer and happier, he may or may not be helped to bear his illness better, but the illness will not be removed ... The higher self will always want to repay Karma in any way it can.[7]

Clearly these are complicated matters and only a detailed study of Steiner's explanations of the working of the laws of karma can enable us to gain a more thorough knowledge, feeling, and understanding of the unique courses of people's lives. Nonetheless the essential point is that *we ourselves*, as spiritual beings, during our sojourn between our last death and our new birth have been active participants in the planning for our present earth life, including the difficulties, or perhaps better said, the challenges, which we shall encounter.

However, in order to better understand why illness and disease have altogether become part and parcel of life on earth, we need to extend our horizon to the wider evolutionary course of humankind in which each of us has also a part to play. This wider perspective is presented, and in great detail, in Steiner's anthroposophy, but we cannot do more than indicate in this chapter a few essential aspects. Importantly, it is true to say that illness and disease are seen in a positive light as the very means whereby a certain balancing and making good of karma, both individually and sometimes also collectively, is enabled to come about. Therefore illness is not simply viewed as an intrinsic evil, to be eliminated at all costs, but rather as an opportunity to bring about necessary changes, compensations, and adjustments. This scenario was, in evolutionary terms, called for because of the interventions of certain adverse elements, or rather actual beings, in the course of humanity's development. These are the specific groups of supersensible beings whom Steiner calls the Luciferic and Ahrimanic spirits. He also often speaks of 'Lucifer' and 'Ahriman' in the singular as the respective leaders of these beings. There are, consequently, some illnesses (the more inflammatory type) which have a marked Luciferic character and others (the sclerotic and hardening illnesses) which have a decidedly Ahrimanic nature. In Lecture IV of *The Manifestations of Karma*, Steiner distinguishes and describes in some detail these two basic types of illness.

Of course, the reality of the matter is usually not as simple and straightforward as we may imagine, so that:

> In anthroposophical medicine, these are the two main types of illness — the feverish and inflammatory on the

> one hand, the degenerative and sclerotic on the other. However, to see any illness as purely one or the other type is almost always an oversimplification, and usually both tendencies are involved. Rheumatoid arthritis, for example, begins with marked inflammation in the joints and they may become red, swollen, painful and hot. As the disease progresses over the years, degenerative tendencies appear, such as chronically deformed joints.[8]

Nonetheless, good health is really the maintaining of *a balance* between these two opposing tendencies. That is, a balance, within the threefold human being, between the cool, catabolic, and hardening tendencies of the Nerve-Sense System on the one hand, and the warm, anabolic, and softening tendencies of the Metabolic-Limb System on the other hand. The natural mediator, and balancer, between head and limbs is then found in the middle Rhythmic System of the breath and heartbeat, as shown in the diagram below.

The Threefold Human Being		
Bodily System	Soul Activity	Physical Effects
Nerve-Sense	Thinking	Cooling, catabolic, hardening
Rhythmic	Feeling	Balancing, mediating
Metabolic-Limb	Willing	Warming, anabolic, softening

In anthroposophy the human being is described as both fourfold and three-fold, depending on whether the four members (Ego, astral, etheric, physical) are under discussion, or the three bodily organic systems and the corresponding three soul-activities.

Macroscopically, in the course of world-evolution, the balance is brought about through the special intervention of another cosmic being, namely Christ, who for three years was incarnated on earth in Jesus of Nazareth from the time of the Baptism in the River Jordan until the Crucifixion on the Cross on Golgotha. Through His unique deed of sacrifice and love, the Cosmic Christ was able to permeate the earth planet as a whole and its etheric life forces, and also all humanity, with new health bestowing forces. On the more microcosmic level we can say that whereas Lucifer brings about illness through the human astral (soul) body and Ahriman through infiltrating the etheric body,[9] the Christ-forces radiating from the Mystery of Golgotha can re-invigorate and strengthen our etheric bodies. In this sense therefore the Christened etheric body is, above all, 'the healer within,' and the means to restore balance and equilibrium in our fourfold constitution. In a lecture given in Nuremberg on December 2, 1911, entitled, *Faith, Love, Hope,* Steiner actually refers to the etheric body as, '*the body of love*.' In our present modern phase of world-evolution and as self-aware thinking people, we can learn to align ourselves consciously with these healing Christ-forces and so strengthen ourselves against the ever-present influences of the Luciferic and Ahrimanic spirits. Indeed, from a higher vantage point, these adversarial spirits have clearly an essential role to play in the development of human beings towards greater independence and true freedom.

Now it has to be admitted that what has been said here will perhaps seem very strange at first sight to those who are unfamiliar with Steiner's teachings. Nonetheless provided we are prepared to keep an open mind on these matters and even overcome certain materialistic prejudices (something which Steiner himself asks us to do), then on reflection it may not seem so very far-fetched after all! We are used nowadays to the thought that we are subject to a wide range of invisible forces and processes, be they gravitational, electrical, magnetic, nuclear, genetic, or whatever. Is it therefore so great a leap for our imagination to also visualize, not only a universe of diverse fields of forces or energies, but also one that includes a diversity of beings — some of whom are below the present level of development of humanity and others far above us? When in the following chapters we will speak of 'healing energies' and also consider the possibility of help from discarnate human and/or higher beings, such as angels, we shall likewise need to keep an open mind for what can strike us, at first, as unusual and novel. In much of the current literature on healing there is an emphasis placed on the recognition of different 'energies' both within the human being and the cosmos. The terms 'energy medicine' and 'energy healing' are becoming commonplace. Also in modern physics the concept of energy, particularly on the subatomic level, has replaced earlier more materialistic theories. We should however bear in mind that Steiner's anthroposophy perceives behind all forces and energies a wide diversity of spiritual beings and not all these beings are well intentioned or benign towards humanity!

The anthroposophical worldview does not therefore see humanity as alone in the vastness of the universe but as part of a complex matrix of beings, energies, and forces, which exist within an evolutionary process which has both meaning and purpose. Neither in the macrocosm nor with the individual person, do events take their course arbitrarily or at random. Laws of life, of destiny and karma, underpin all that proceeds. And yet, in spite of this, there is still room for real freedom, choice, and creativity. This again reflects the objectively Christian aspect which permeates Steiner's anthroposophy and which differentiates it from any hard and fast dogma of fate and predestination.

Karmic laws and necessities can be met in a variety of ways, and the Christ-Impulse is, above all, an impulse of freedom and love. This is best expressed in Steiner's own words when he writes:

> This is the mystery of all future evolution: that our knowledge and everything we do out of a true understanding of evolution sow seeds that must ripen into love. The greater the power of love that comes into being, the more we will be able to accomplish creatively on behalf of the future.[10]

It cannot be emphasized too strongly how important are Steiner's comprehensive and detailed descriptions of the course of world-evolution gleaned from his reading of the supersensible Akashic Record or Chronicle, in which all events have been inscribed and preserved. Only by a thorough understanding of humanity's past can we strive to fashion the future with true vision and purpose.

The ultimate goal of earth evolution is to bring about a process of spiritualization and of moral and ethical development based on the transforming power of unconditional love. Clearly we still have far to go along this way!

From what has been touched upon in this chapter as a background, we will now proceed to try to gain a deepened understanding of the reality of spiritual healing in the light of anthroposophy.

3. Spiritual Science and Spiritual Healing

The most clear and direct reference by Steiner to healing by the laying-on-of-hands is found in a lecture which he gave in Zurich on 25 February 1911 and entitled, in English, *The Work of the Ego in Childhood*. In this lecture Steiner describes how in the young child, up to the age of three or three and a half years, there exists a sort of 'telephonic connection' between its own being, or Ego, and the divine-spiritual beings or hierarchies. This initial intimate connection to the spiritual world in which the child's own spiritual being, its Ego, works from outside onto the formation and development of its own small body and, in particular, the brain, is severed when the dawn of self-consciousness arises in the child at round about three years of age.[1]

Steiner says that the human being may be thought of as twofold, namely, the one we see during the first three and a half years, and the one we see, in possession of individual self-consciousness, for the rest of his life. He refers to the first being, in the language of esotericism, as the 'Son of God' (because he is directly connected with the higher hierarchies), and the other being as the 'Son of Man,' in which the forces of the Ego now work from within outwards.

Steiner points out that:

> The son of God who is pre-eminently active for the first three and a half years of life embraces all the vitalising forces, [and] stimulates the human being to pour these life-giving forces in greater and ever greater

> measure into his organism. In comparison with those in an older person these forces are also health-giving, strengthening factors.[2]

Rudolf Steiner goes on to describe that these vitalizing health-giving spiritual forces can be awakened *consciously* in later life through, for example, our spiritual strivings and our efforts to acquire living ideas and conceptions of the higher worlds. A little further on in the lecture Steiner then makes a very clear and specific reference to healing through the laying-on-of-hands, and I will therefore quote the whole passage in which this specific reference occurs.

> It is the very best part of manhood that we have within us during these early years, only the solid physical body prevents us from using these forces then to the fullest extent. Even if someone in his later years succeeds in developing them to a special extent, he cannot transform his physical body which is by no means as pliable as wax. But if through esoteric wisdom he is able to use these forces to the full, their power streams through the tips of his fingers, and he acquires the gift of healing, of health-bestowal through the laying on of hands — if, that is to say, these spiritual forces are still active. They can no longer transform his body but when they stream out from him they bring about healing.[3]

What then are these 'spiritual forces' which, via the hands, can bring about healing? What is their source? It becomes clear in the rest of the lecture that these forces are bestowed upon us by the Being of Christ Himself and that, whether a person is conscious of it or not, those same vitalizing Christ-forces which radiated within him in earliest childhood continue to live on within him in the depths of his own soul. Whether or not a person actually professes a Christian faith, it remains an objective fact of world evolution that:

> Christ lives within him and will do so in an ever wider sense through all the following incarnations.

We therefore see in this lecture given in Zurich in 1911 that Rudolf Steiner clearly acknowledges the reality of healing through the laying-on-of-hands, and that he makes clear to us that the spiritual forces which flow from the healer are nothing else but inner Christ-forces. Or, to put it another way, we could say that the great World-Healer can indeed work through us when, as conscious adults, we actively strive towards the Spirit.

Although Steiner does not use the word 'Love' in this particular context we understand, both from spiritual science and from the Gospels, that it was through Christ's Deeds on Golgotha (the Death and Resurrection) that the impulse and power of unconditional love flowed as a transformative force into earthly evolution, and that He clearly wished that this impulse should be realized more and more in the hearts and souls of human beings on earth.

In the impressive Farewell Discourses in the fifteenth chapter of the Gospel of St John, Christ-Jesus says:

> If you dwell in me, and my words dwell in you, ask what you will, and you shall have it. This is my Father's glory, that you may bear fruit in plenty and so be my disciples. As the Father has loved me, so I have loved you. Dwell in my love. If you heed my commands, you will dwell in my love, as I have heeded my Father's commands and dwell in his love.

> I have spoken thus to you, so that my joy may be in you, and your joy complete. This is my commandment: love one another, as I have loved you.[5]

Therefore I believe it is fully justified to call those existential health-bestowing Christ-forces, which can be called to life through the earnest spiritual striving of a healer, forces of selfless love. This assertion is, I believe, supported when we turn to another very clear reference to the reality of what, in one published translation, Steiner calls 'psychic' healings. Whether this is precisely the same as what, in this book, is meant by the term 'spiritual' healing we must still explore further.

It should however first be pointed out once more, and particularly so in our contemporary pluralistic and multifaith society, that the objective Christ-Impulse, and the Being of Christ Himself, is understood in Steiner's anthroposophy as pivotal to the whole course of world evolution. It is inclusive not exclusive, in the very same sense that selfless love knows no boundaries of race, colour, or religion. Indeed in the course of world evolution that same Sun-Spirit who as 'the Christ' incarnated in the body of Jesus of Nazareth, was revered in earlier, pre-Christian, cultures under different names. In ancient India as Vishvakarman, in ancient Persia as Ahura-Mazdao, in ancient Egypt as Osiris, and in Greece as Apollo.[6]

In the year 1910 Steiner gave a series of eleven lectures in Hamburg, entitled, in English, *The Manifestations of Karma*. In several of these lectures he speaks about the nature of illness and diseases in the light of an understanding of karmic laws and relationships, and also in regard to certain Luciferic and Ahrimanic influences, i.e. the influence of specific spiritual entities which Steiner refers to again and again in his anthroposophical teachings. It is however in the tenth lecture, where he turns to the theme of, 'Free will and karma in the future of human evolution,' that he throws some very helpful light on the reality underlying *psychic* healings. In this particular lecture Steiner speaks of the deeper nature of material existence and also of the essential nature of soul existence. He makes a point of emphasizing to his listeners how far removed from the science and thought of the present time (i.e. in 1911) are the particular results of spiritual research which he will now describe.

Likewise I would also urge readers of today to study Steiner's lecture in its entirety in order to be able to place the selected extracts which follow, in their proper context.

He says:

> There is a fundamental essence of our material earth existence out of which all matter only comes into being by a condensing process, and to the question: What is this fundamental substance of our earth existence? Spiritual Science gives the answer: 'Every substance upon the earth is condensed light.'
>
> ... All matter is, in its essence, light ... If we look at the material human body, that also, inasmuch as it consists of matter, is nothing but a substance woven of light.[7]

Does not this surprising result of spiritual-scientific research now appear much more credible in the light of modern physics and quantum theory?[8]

Having dealt with the underlying nature of material existence he then turns to the other question of: What does the soul consist? And in answer, and again on the basis of the methods of investigation of spiritual science, Steiner says that:

> ... just as all matter is compressed light, so all the different phenomena of the soul upon earth are modifications, are manifold transformations of that which must be called, if we truly realise the fundamental meaning of the word: love.[9]

In the human being there is then a wonderful intermingling of these two most fundamental elements so that we find that:

> ... his outer bodily part is woven out of light, and his inner soul is woven spiritually out of love.[10]

Steiner then proceeds to describe how in the two main types of illnesses and disease (Luciferic or Ahrimanic), appropriate therapeutic help may be given either from the realm of matter (i.e. from light) via *medicinal remedies*, derived from the Kingdoms of nature, or from the realm of the soul (i.e. from love) by means of *psychic healing* methods. In regard to the latter I would now like to quote the relevant passages at length.

> All those acts of healing dependent upon what we may call a 'psychic healing process' must have the characteristic that love is part of the process. In some form or other all psychic healing depends on a stream of love, which we pour into another person as a balsam. All that is done in this domain must finally be traced back to love. All arises from the impulse of love, from simpler processes of healing, to that which is often, in amateur fashion, called 'magnetic healing.' What does the healer communicate to the one to be healed? It is, to use an expression of physics, an 'interchange of tensions.' Certain processes in the etheric body of the

> healer create with the person to be healed a sort of polarity. Polarity arises just as it would arise in an abstract sense, when one kind of electricity, say positive, is produced and then the corresponding electricity — the negative — appears. Thus polarities are created, and this act must be conceived as emanating from sacrifice. One evokes in oneself a process which is not intended to be significant to oneself only, for then one could call forth one process only; in this case, however, the process is intended in addition to induce a polarity in another person, and this polarity, which naturally depends upon a contact, between the healer and the person to be healed, is, in the fullest sense of the word, the sacrifice of a force which is no other than the transmuted action of love. That is what is really active in these psychic healings — a transmuted power of love. We must clearly understand that without this fundamental love-force the healing will not lead to the right goal ... In that which is considered as the technique of the healing process, even to the way in which the movements of the hands are made, and technically reduced to a system, we have the reflection of a sacrificial act.

And:

> Since the soul consists fundamentally of love, we can assist with psychic factors ... Because love is the fundamental essence of the soul, we may, indeed, influence the direction of Karma.[11]

Following these descriptions Steiner goes on to speak about healing from the realm of substance (light) by means of remedies derived from the animal, vegetable, or mineral kingdoms. He then sums up the *two directions* from which healing help can be given by saying:

> Through his connection with the surrounding world, man can be helped from two different sides — on the one hand by bringing him transmuted love from the psychic methods of healing and on the other hand by bringing him transmuted light in various ways by those processes which are connected with external methods of healing. Everything that can be done is brought about either by inner psychic means — by love — or by the external means of densified light ... [12]

And a little further on:

> We either draw the remedies out of our surroundings, out of the condensed light, or out of our own soul by the healing loving act, the sacrificial act, and we then heal with the soul forces obtained from love.[13]

Perhaps it would be more true to the spirit of the healing act or service, to imagine what Steiner calls 'the sacrificial act' as rather, 'a making sacred.' That is to say, the creation of a *Sacred Space* between the healer and his patient in which forces of healing can rightly be given and received.

From all that has been presented in this chapter we can see that, without a shadow of a doubt, Rudolf Steiner acknowledged the reality of spiritual and/or psychic (soul) healing given via *direct contact* between the healer and his patient. Nonetheless there is, I believe, a need to try to gain still greater clarification about what appear to be different kinds of non-material healing methods, in order that a real understanding of *spiritual* healing can be gained. We will therefore turn to this task in the next chapter.

4. Spiritual, Psychic and Magnetic Healing

As I have said earlier, spiritual healers see themselves as willing channels for the flow of healing energies to reach those who are sick or suffering. That they also foster in themselves a compassionate and loving attitude to those in need of help goes without saying. Healers must strive to overcome in themselves the all too human characteristics of egoism, pride, power, and self-aggrandisement, in order to become purer and finer channels for the transmission of the healing energies. This will necessitate some form of inner work and spiritual development.

We have seen in Chapter 3 that Rudolf Steiner clearly recognized the reality and validity of soul-spiritual methods of healing. However what is not so clear is whether Steiner's remarks support the image of the spiritual healer as a channel for *external* spiritual healing energies to flow through, or as a person who is able to transmit psychic healing forces, i.e. forces of love, from his or her own *inner* soul reserves.

Now this issue, or question, about outer or inner healing forces or energies and the healer's role in relationship to them may, on a higher level of being, be seen as not an either/or situation but rather simply two sides of the same coin, which do not contradict but rather supplement each other. After all, the forces of unconditional pure love, that is to say the actual Christ-forces, live *both* within the depths of the human soul and also in the cosmos. Christ encompasses with His being of love, both the individual and the universal. Therefore when Steiner speaks as he did in the single lecture of 25 February 1911 of those inner Christ-imbued vitalizing forces which can be consciously cultivated in later life (i.e. beyond early childhood), and thereby lead to the gift of healing, of health-bestowal through the laying-on-of-hands, and when in the lecture series of May 1910 he says that 'In some form or other all psychic healing depends on a stream of love, which we pour into the other person as a balsam'[1] he may very well be referring to *the same* higher source of healing power. This power, which flows through the healer's hands in direct contact-healing may therefore be seen both as an inner and as an outer spiritual force or energy. The terms 'inner' and 'outer' probably do not have that same meaning of spatial division and separation on the higher levels of existence, i.e. soul and spiritual, as when they are applied on the physical material level only. The inevitable spatial separateness which incarnation into a material body imposes upon us in the physical world is clearly overcome on the soul and spiritual levels when we are, literally, fully united with others in sympathy and love.

But, for all this, and for the sake of doing justice to the reality of spiritual healing *per se*, I believe there does need to be a genuine distinction drawn when comparing this with so-called 'magnetic healing.' This distinction is clearly made by Harry Edwards in his book, *A Guide to the Understanding and Practice of Spiritual Healing* and is based on his forty years' experience as a spiritual healer. Edwards writes:

> Magnetic healing is a direct inheritance from Mesmer. It is the ability to direct to a patient some of the healer's own abundance of natural vitality or cosmic strength... When a magnetic healer gives of his vital-

> ity to a number of patients then he is liable to feel a sense of depletion and consciously needs to replenish his energies.[2]

And, a little further on, he states:

> Magnetic healing can be very helpful to a patient who is weak — but this is *not* spiritual healing. The energies do not come from a spirit source — they are of physical origin only. Magnetic healing and spiritual healing can merge, but it is not possible to draw any dividing line between them.[3]

Edwards' assertion that it is, 'not possible to draw any dividing line between them' seems puzzling since he is clear that there is a clear distinction to be made between these two forms of healing. However it seems likely that he is referring here to the possibility of a spontaneous merging from these *two sources of energy* when the healer is relating to his patient for he also points out that:

> Most healers have the faculty of imparting this strength to a patient [i.e. from their own natural vitality], as they blend in with him when they direct strength to flow from themselves into the patient. If a healer feels at all depleted after treating patients, it may well mean that he has given more than he should of his own strength.[4]

Quite recently I came upon an interesting and precise example of the effect of magnetic healing upon the healer. In a conversation with the mother of one of our pupils at the Sheiling School she described to me how her partner had always had a certain natural healing gift. He sensed if someone was ill or had pain and had then the urge to put his hands on the person. His hands became very warm, even hot. However after doing this he himself felt weakened, as if drained of energy and would need to rest. Here then we can see a clear difference between the magnetic and the spiritual healer.

However when Edwards speaks of the vitality of the magnetic healer and that the energies used in magnetic healing 'are of physical origin only' it appears that, unlike Steiner, he does not clearly distinguish between the physical body and the etheric body as the two interpenetrating members of the human being's fourfold constitution.

Greater light is thrown on the specific nature and process of magnetic healing by Rudolf Steiner in answer to a question that was put to him during a course of lectures which he gave to young doctors, in January 1924. However before quoting from this source it is helpful to once again refer briefly to the fourfold constitution of the human being as described in Steiner's anthroposophy. It is very important to be clear about Steiner's precise use of terminology, e.g. the term Ego, because the same words are sometimes used very differently by other people!

According to Steiner's teachings the human being consists of four distinct members; namely the physical body, the etheric body, the astral body, and the Ego. The etheric body is that which imparts life-forces to the physical mineral body throughout a person's life on earth. At death the etheric body separates from the corpse after a few days and, because of this, natural processes of physical dissolution then ensue. Whilst incarnated in our physical body not only do we live and grow, like the plants, but we also enjoy a conscious inner soul-life with our thoughts, feelings and impulses of will. This inner life is made possible, says Steiner, by the inclusion of our astral, or soul body. However in addition to an active soul-life we have as human beings a clear awareness of ourselves as distinct individuals, in other words we have self-consciousness. This is thanks to the fourth member of our constitution, the Ego. While our astral body is of the nature of soul, our Ego is related to the world of the Spirit. Our fourfold constitution therefore provides us with the sheaths in which, on earth, we exist as beings of body, soul, and spirit. With this in mind let us now look, and in full, at precisely how Rudolf Steiner answered the very *specific question* which was put to him at the beginning of the seventh lecture of the *Course for Young Doctors*, on 8 January 1924, namely:

Are there definite exercises for strengthening the so-called magnetic healing forces, and what are these exercises?

> *Steiner*: This, of course, necessitates a few words about the nature of the forces of magnetic healing. The magnetic healing forces are forces which play, essentially, between the etheric body of the one person and the etheric body of the other. You must picture to yourselves that the efficacy of what goes by the name of healing magnetism is based on the following. Suppose somebody has a very strong character, that is to say, it is possible for him to unfold his will very strongly. Indications can be given to such a person. I can, for instance, say to him when he is suffering from some illness or other: every morning at eleven o'clock you should think about the sun; think that the sun warms your head first, and then that the warmth of your head passes to your upper arm, lower arm, hands, so that your own power is strengthened; then, when you have strengthened your own power, try to make a clear mental image of

what you feel about your illness, in order, then, through the power of your will, to get rid of it. This procedure may help, when the illness is not connected with damage to a specific organ, whereby the damage can naturally extend itself to all four parts of the elemental body: the solid, fluid, aeriform, and warmth elements. Although I do not say that it will invariably help, for there is always something problematic about these things.

Through the indications given him, the astral body of the patient has been stimulated. The indication which he has put into practice, this picturing of the sun, the warmth in his head, and so on, which has still further strengthened his will — this has worked upon his astral body. The astral body has worked upon his etheric body and the etheric body in turn has worked in a healing way on his physical body and has been able to adjust, to nullify the trouble which is not a deep, organic one. It cannot be said that such healing can only occur in what modern medicine calls 'functional' disturbance in contrast to organic disturbance where there is an actual disturbance of the organs themselves. This difference is, as a matter of fact, quite inexact. It is impossible to say where functional disturbances cease and organic disturbances begin. In functional diseases there are always slight organic disturbances as well, only these latter cannot be proved by the crude methods of physiology and pathology today. In a case like that which I have described, we are not applying the forces of magnetic healing, but we are calling upon the patient's power to heal himself and this method, when it can be used, is the best, under all circumstances. We thereby strengthen the patient's will, as we make him well.[5]

4. *Spiritual, Psychic and Magnetic Healing*

In this first part of Steiner's response to the questioner he is therefore describing, effectively, a method of *self-healing*. This is achieved through willed mental visualization which stimulates the person's own astral body and which, in turn, strengthens his own etheric body which directly affects his own physical organism. However, Steiner then goes on to describe a somewhat different scenario:

> The following is also possible. Out of our own astral body, without the patient exerting his own will, we can influence our own etheric body in such a way that *our own etheric body works upon the etheric body of the patient* in the same way as, in the previous case, the astral body worked. *It is in this that healing magnetism consists* [Author's italics]. The magnetic healer does this unconsciously; he influences his own etheric body with his astral body. Instinctively, he can then so direct the forces he unfolds that as he passes them on to the patient they strengthen the patient's forces. You must realise that if it is to be a question of healing, the magnetic healer must use means that are able, somehow, to bring it about. If we have a patient who is weak, of whose will we can expect nothing, the forces of healing magnetism may sometimes be applied. But I want to say, with emphasis, that magnetic healing forces are pretty problematical and are not equally useful in all cases. The instinctive faculty of activating one's own astral body in order thereby to influence one's own etheric body and then work over into the etheric body of the patient — this instinctive faculty is an individual one. There are people in whom it is strong, others in whom it is weak, others who do not possess it at all. There are people who are, by nature, magnetic healers — certainly there are. But the important thing is this, that the faculty is,

as a rule, of limited duration. The natural magnetic healers have this magnetism, as it is called. When they begin to apply it, it may work very well; after a time it begins to wane, and later on it often happens that magnetic healers, after this faculty has died down in them, go on acting as if they still had it, and then charlatanism begins.

This is the precarious element when magnetic healing becomes a profession. This kind of healing really cannot be made into a profession. That is what must be said about it.

The process of magnetic healing — when a person has the faculty for it — is only unconditionally effective when it is carried out with genuine compassion for the patient, a compassion that goes right down into one's organism. If you practice magnetic healing with a real love for the patient, then it cannot be done as a profession. If real love exists it will always be able to lead to something good, if no trouble arises from another side. But it can only be done on occasions when Karma leads us to a person whom we are able, out of love, to help; then the outer sign may be a laying on of the hand, or a stroking and then what is happening is that the astral body is passing on its forces to the etheric body which then works upon the etheric body of the other person.

Something must still be said from another aspect about what goes on here. The healing always proceeds from the astral body, either from the patient's own astral body or from the astral body of the magnetiser. The reverse is the case in therapy where medicaments are used. When you give medicaments you introduce into the physical body substances which then work partly upon the inner forces and partly upon the rhythm of the physical body in such a way that the

> etheric body of the patient is influenced. The healing always proceeds from the etheric body. If you influence the etheric body from the astral body — which is a psychical healing — this lies in the realm of magnetic healing and is somewhat problematic, having a humanitarian, social element in it, something to do with the relations of one human being to another. Rational therapy must proceed from intervention by means of medicaments which proceed from the physical body and pass into the etheric body. Always, however, the healing proceeds from the etheric body. It is a complete illusion that the physical body, when it has become ill, can itself bring about any healing. The physical body has, precisely, the basis of illness within it, and the cause of healing must always come from the etheric body.[6]

Steiner therefore provides us with a very thorough and detailed explanation of the process of magnetic healing based on an understanding of the fourfold human constitution. Healing forces can indeed be directly transferred from the etheric body of the magnetic healer to the etheric body of the patient in the same, or similar, sense that Harry Edwards also describes. But is this really the same as spiritual healing? Edwards maintains it is not, and other experienced spiritual healers would agree with him.

Unfortunately, to my knowledge, no one asked Rudolf Steiner a specific question about *spiritual* healing, in contrast to magnetic healing. But we do know that when he spoke about the acquisition of the gift of healing, of health-bestowal through the laying-on-of-hands, in his lecture of 1911 entitled *The Work of the Ego in Childhood*, he was clearly pointing to the activity of the spiritual forces of the Ego imbued with the healing forces of the Christ Being.

This certainly suggests that the source of healing forces, or energies, is not restricted only to the levels of the etheric or the astral bodies, but can also flow directly from the level of the Ego, i.e. from the Spirit, in distinction to the psychic level of the astral or soul. As Edwards stated there may well be a certain 'merging' of the levels of healing influence but, nonetheless, spiritual healing is not the same as magnetic healing, nor, it seems, is it identical with so-called psychic healings. The internationally known healer and medium, Betty Shine, who sadly died in April 2002, describes in detail basic methods of psychic healing in her book, *Mind Magic — the key to the universe*. These methods call upon the exercise of a person's own active imagination and the use of strong visualizations to help bring about self-healing processes. However I believe that *the common thread* which can indeed link all three types of healing is the power of unconditional love and compassion.

We can now summarize the differentiations which have been made in this chapter in the following simple diagram.

Subtle Energy Level		Type of Healing
Ego	→	Spiritual Healing
Astral	→	Psychic Healing
Etheric	→	Magnetic Healing

Without becoming unduly dogmatic I also believe it is important when attempting to clearly differentiate between different forms of subtle energy healing, to perceive what level of consciousness is involved on the part of the healer. Similarly we should learn to differentiate between psychic abilities and spirituality. A person could be very psychic but not necessarily very spiritual in their striving and ideals, or vice versa. Steiner makes it very clear in his description of magnetic healing that this ability is both natural and instinctive to the magnetic healer. That is to say it is largely, or completely, unconscious. In contrast however, the spiritual healer should act in wakeful consciousness as a willing channel for healing forces or energies. In spiritual healing therefore a much higher level of awareness is involved than is the case in magnetic healing. This higher level of awareness can be acquired, and developed, through training and practice. This training (see Chapter 8) will include practice in spiritual attunement and also meditation in one form or another.

The difference between instinctive magnetic healing ability and conscious spiritual healing might perhaps be compared to the distinction between an atavistic form of natural clairvoyance and an acquired clairvoyance that has been systematically and consciously developed by following an inner path of soul training. Even when a person has a certain natural gift for healing, (or for clairvoyance for that matter), the further development, control, and conscious application of this potential should, I believe, be attained in our modern times through individual freedom and decision. Once this decision has been made then definite ethical and moral responsibilities must also be taken on board in full awareness. Therefore the two years of initial training required of probationer healers by the various UK healing organizations is underpinned by a formal 'Code of Conduct' and by clear written procedures for the self-regulation and discipline of its members. I think that it is the level of awareness and consciousness of the *spiritual healer* which distinguishes his or her practice from the other kinds of non-material healing methods which we have considered.

Far from being atavistic in nature it seems to me that consciously acquired ability in spiritual healing is likely to be futuristic!

5. The Work of the Healer

Is spiritual healing a reality? Does it work?

Through experience and practice I am convinced that these two questions can be answered in the affirmative.

While the understanding of just *how* spiritual healing works is considered in other chapters of this book, my own philosophy in regard to its application and practice is unashamedly pragmatic. The old adage, 'The proof of the pudding is in the eating,' sums up eloquently my attitude to spiritual healing. If someone asks me for healing, or else accepts my offer to give them healing, then we shall simply see what happens; perhaps not immediately, but, in the course of time. And, therefore, as another traditional saying goes, 'Nothing ventured, nothing gained!' Exactly what may be gained from the healing-process for any particular complaint or condition will have to be viewed entirely individually. No promises or guarantees of cures can ever be given but, on the other hand, spiritual healing is very likely to bring the sufferer some benefit in one form or another and also on one or more levels of his/her constitution, be it physical, emotional, mental, or spiritual. Whilst it is of course always gratifying to see 'good results' benefiting the recipient of healing, the healer must guard against any form of vanity or self aggrandisement in this respect. He or she is after all simply a willing instrument, or mediator, for the healing forces. Moreover the good results hoped for may not show themselves at once but can take weeks or months, as the process of healing gradually continues over repeated sessions.

Examples, gleaned from my own practice, will now be given to substantiate the claim that spiritual healing is a reality and that it works. People's names have been changed to preserve confidentiality and anonymity, but all else is true to what took place at the time.

Jim

My wife told me that Jim, a friend of ours, was having a lot of pain with his back. I decided to offer him some healing for this and phoned his home. Jim's wife took my message and said she would relay this offer to him. A week or two passed without any word back from Jim.

I have learnt, through hard experience, not to press healing on anyone, even if I feel fairly confident that it could be of help to them. However, as it happened, Jim himself then took the initiative to ring me up and ask for healing. I was able to go over to his home that very evening, and it was clear to see that he still had his painful back problem. The doctor had diagnosed a slipped disc and recommended rest as the best, and perhaps only, form of treatment. If the condition didn't ease up, after some months, the possibility of an operation could be considered. Meantime painkillers had been prescribed to at least give some temporary relief from the often severe pain, and to enable Jim to get some sleep at night.

Jim hobbled from his sitting room into the kitchen to sit down on an upright wooden chair. He didn't use the walking stick, which I had noticed in the hallway when I arrived, for this short but painful journey. I sat myself down next to him and simply placed my hands on his lower back in the area where the pain seemed to be located and inwardly asked for help to be given him. Jim had not received this form of healing before but, given his state, he was more than open to try anything which might bring some relief. The healing session in the kitchen lasted perhaps fifteen minutes. Jim felt relatively relaxed and peaceful. I suggested he tried standing up and seeing how his back felt. He did so and, to his great surprise, he felt much better and was now able to straighten himself up. Just at this moment Jim's wife happened to come into the kitchen, having returned from a meeting elsewhere. She was also very surprised to see him standing upright as he was, and remarked that she hadn't seen him being able to do this for a couple of weeks. Over the following three days I went across to his home to give Jim further healing sessions. Each time he experienced a relaxation of tension and relief from pain.

After the fourth such session Jim went to see his GP. The doctor was pleased with his progress and arranged to see him again in two weeks. The next day I saw Jim once more. He confirmed he was now feeling, and sleeping, better. Five days later we met up again and he told me he had during the day driven his car for some two hours! By the evening his back was again rather painful!

Jim received three further healing sessions. At the third of these, and after a grand total of eight sessions, he declared that his back was, at present, better. I did not see Jim again and he continued to make a good recovery and was able, with care, to resume his normal day-to-day activities. However this was not the end of the story.

Some four-and-a-half months later, in April 2003, Jim unfortunately suffered a recurrence of his slipped disc. There had, it seems, been no obvious cause which had triggered this very painful and disabling state. Naturally he felt quite dejected about this. On the day it occurred Jim received an injection from the doctor to relieve his pain and then (without this time delaying asking for a week or two), he contacted me to request healing. I went to see him, at home in the evening, and at the end of the session suggested that he would let me know if, and when, he wanted further sessions.

The next day I heard no word from Jim and therefore assumed, optimistically, that things were looking up for him: that no news was good news. However, just to be on the safe side, I decided on the following day to ring him up and ask how he was feeling. I was disappointed to learn that yesterday he had been in a lot of pain in the evening, but he hadn't phoned me! Anyway I offered to come over again and see him. He accepted this and, at the end of the session, I once again left it to him to contact me if he wanted further healing. One day later Jim phoned for healing. On this occasion he said he had experienced a very strong pull on his head, soon after the start of the session, when I had lightly placed my hands there as usual. In fact the pull had been so powerful that he had almost asked me to remove them!

Jim received healing over the next six days. He felt the benefit from this each time, especially through becoming very peaceful and relaxed. In all we had nine sessions, beginning immediately his back trouble had again flared up, with Jim only occasionally taking painkillers. A further two sessions followed and, on the second of these, he declared that he had resumed jogging! He still had a bit of an ache in his back, but no pain as such. No further healing was required. It had taken just over two weeks to alleviate the problem, though such a condition could perhaps, without healing, have taken months to right itself. At any event Jim had no doubts that spiritual healing had worked for him, and he was still jogging a month and a half later!

Of course it may be that the weakness in his back will be the cause of more problems in the future. We certainly hope not, but, if this does happen, I suspect that Jim will waste no time in requesting further healing help.

Postcard

Floris Books
15 Harrison Gardens
Edinburgh
EH11 1SH
United Kingdom

If you are interested in other publications from Floris Books, please return this card with your name and address.

I am interested in the following subjects:

- ☐ C Celtic
- ☐ R Religion
- ☐ S Science
- ☐ H Health & parenting
- ☐ J Children's books
- ☐ A Crafts & activities

Floris Books

PC-0107

Name ______________________
Surname

Address ______________________

____

____

____
Postcode

- ☐ Please send me your catalogue ONCE
- ☐ Please send me your catalogue REGULARLY
- ☐ Please E-mail me about new books in future

E-mail: ______________________

If you are in North America, our distributor, Anthroposophic Press, will send their catalogue to you.

I found this card in: ______________________
Book title

Sandra and Billy

Sandra came to see me for healing. She suffered sometimes from severe headaches. She had not received spiritual healing before.

Sandra felt after this first session that the experience was beneficial and had been very relaxing. She said that she would come again.

Two weeks later I saw Sandra for a second healing session. She also brought her young son, Billy, with her. Sandra said that she had had two headaches since she saw me last. Nonetheless, she felt that the healing had helped her. On this same occasion Sandra also asked for some healing for six-year-old Billy who suffered from asthma.

Billy sat peacefully for this short session, with the healing being directed especially over his chest area.

A week later mother and son came to see me again. Sandra received her third healing session. Although, as usual, I felt warmth in my hands whilst transmitting the healing energy, Sandra said that, today, she did not experience so much in the way of warmth. Instead she felt more a movement of energy; sometimes it felt heavy. I wondered if this indicated a shifting of something that needed to be moved? Last week, she remarked, she had had a high temperature which was very unusual for her. I felt therefore that we would just have to wait and see what would happen with her and, naturally, hope for positive results.

Once again Billy also received a short healing session, with me simply first placing my hands on his head and then over his chest, i.e. one hand on his front and the other at his back. Sandra said that she had not needed to use the ventilator at all this past week for his asthma, which was good news.

As it happened I did not see Sandra or Billy for healing

again. However some four months later I heard that Billy had been keeping free of asthma! Thereafter I enquired from time to time how he was getting on and, some two years since he had come for healing, his father told me that the asthma was no longer a problem and that both he and his wife had been impressed with the positive change which had taken place. However I never heard how Sandra's headaches were!

Katherine

Katherine had, unfortunately, cracked her left shoulder joint. Seeing her arm in a sling I offered to give her some healing for it. She accepted, and felt that this was beneficial.

As it transpired Katherine also suffered from multiple sclerosis (MS) and, when I realized this, I again offered her healing. She came for a total of thirteen sessions over a period of six months.

I felt that Katherine was very receptive to the healing energy. She seemed to soak it up like a sponge with water, and said she could feel the beneficial effects from each session. This was particularly so in improving her energy levels, and there was often a marked difference in her vitality from the start to the end of a session. In one such session I had not seen Katherine for healing for about six weeks, owing to intervening holidays. She said she was feeling worn out and that she had a headache. After the healing, Katherine reported feeling better and her headache had gone!

When she arrived for another session she once more felt depleted. Moreover over the past three weeks she was having problems focussing her eyes. (I hadn't seen her for over a month.) After the healing she said she felt better and when I saw her two weeks later she told me that her eyes were okay again, having improved the morning following the previous healing session. A week later she confirmed that her eyes were still alright.

For some reason, after six months, Katherine did not come to see me any more for healing, in spite of the fact that she had again and again clearly felt the beneficial effects of the healing sessions. As far as I was concerned I was willing and open to continue to see Katherine, however I did not want her to feel under any pressure or obligation to come for healing. This has always to be a matter for personal choice and free decision. Optimistically, I simply hope that Katherine has continued to feel better and that her MS is in remission. As a healer I have decided to adopt the positive attitude that if someone discontinues to see me for healing then they are probably feeling better than they were and, therefore, no longer ask for it. I hope I'm right!

Mary

Spiritual healing I believe does work on different levels within a human being. In that sense it is holistic and can therefore sometimes meet a person's health needs on the spiritual, mental, emotional, and physical levels.

Mary was, so to speak, a case in point probably having needs on all of these different levels after an accident which left her with complicated fractures in her left leg. She gladly accepted the regular healing which I offered her and gained benefit from it in various ways.

Physically her leg made a good and steady recovery and after approximately some four months from the accident her physiotherapist confirmed that Mary's foot and knee had recovered remarkably well and also quickly. However in parallel with the actual physical healing of her leg, Mary also clearly benefited emotionally and psychologically through having the regular healing sessions. These sessions brought relaxation and inner peace and confidence, as well as helping to relieve physical pain and give improved movement and flexibility. Mary's recovery provides a good example of the need to treat the whole person and not only a particular area of the body or just one level of our spiritual/soul/physical constitution.

Mary's accident occurred in the early autumn but by the following spring the leg was better and functioning nearly normally. Needless to say, Mary had received help medically as well as through spiritual healing, to strengthen her body's own natural healing forces.

Fred

Fred came to see me after I had mentioned to him that healing might be able to help him. He suffered from discomfort, and sometimes a lot of pain, on his left side as the after-effect of an operation he had had two years previously for a lung condition. Medically, it seemed, there was little that could be done to relieve his discomfort.

When Fred came for his second healing session he said that he had already benefited from the first session of the day before. I therefore suggested to him that he should see how things were going and let me know if he wanted further healing next week.

In fact, Fred saw me on a weekly basis over the following three weeks. As a result of these healings he said that his left side had been 'easier' though he still got some 'twinges' in the mornings.

Fred went to see his doctor. She felt that tension in his left shoulder was at least partly to blame for his aches and pains. Therefore, in subsequent healing sessions, one aim was to help reduce his bodily tension and to bring increased relaxation. Fred received three further healing sessions after his visit to the doctor. In the sessions he felt warmth coming through my hands (a common experience in spiritual healing), and a releasing of tension in his shoulders. I had also suggested that he practised, at times of his own choosing, some 'characterized breathing' as it has been described by Harry Edwards.[1] The aim of this simple breathing technique is to imagine to consciously take in health-giving vitalizing forces on the in-breath and to exhale tension, tiredness, pain, and any toxic waste products with the outbreath.

On the last occasion, the eighth, when he came for healing, Fred said that he had found the benefit of doing 'characterized breathing' and of learning to relax more. About two weeks later, when I happened to see him on his way to work, I asked how he was getting on. Fred replied that he was 'a changed man' and that he had no further aches or pains on his left side. More than a year later he continues to be amazed about the betterment he obtained through spiritual healing.

In Fred's case the healing process had been spread over approximately two months. Just as it is not possible to guarantee a cure with spiritual healing, it is also not possible to say beforehand how long may be needed for an individual to gain the maximum benefit that is sought for. However it is true to say that sometimes, as in the case of Billy with his asthma, or in the case of Joan as described below, very positive results can occur quickly.

Joan

When, at her request, Joan came for a healing session she told me that she had had a pain in her left leg for a long time. Healing was given on this first visit, especially for her left knee and foot. A day or two later when I asked her how her leg was she said that she had found definite benefit from the healing. In fact the previous pain had disappeared! Further enquiries some weeks and months later confirmed this good result.

About nine months later Joan came to see me again. This time because of her painful right arm, quite possibly due to some muscle strain. She had, apparently, suffered with aches and pain from this arm already for a month before asking now for some healing for it! Another month passed before she came for a second healing session. She said that the arm had improved since the earlier healing but recently it had again become painful. Healing was given and, just less than a month later, Joan came once again. The arm was unfortunately still playing up despite visits to the doctor. Joan then received three healing sessions over some twelve days.

In giving her healing I felt a lot of warmth over her right shoulder, and, by the third of these sessions, Joan felt that her arm was indeed improving gradually.

Perhaps if she had come for healing as soon as the painful condition had started and had then received healing regularly (say weekly), a good result might have been achieved much quicker? At any event Joan's case illustrates that each complaint, even with the same person, must be dealt with as it arises and can respond very differently in terms of the time taken for optimum relief and recovery.

Margaret

Margaret had asked me for healing following the positive and quick results which spiritual healing had had on her friend's painful foot after just a few sessions with me. In fact his foot had completely recovered, although medical treatment had proved ineffective.

Margaret suffered from hiatus hernia which resulted in acid reflux from the stomach and caused a very unpleasant burning sensation, i.e. heartburn. She also had a left knee that was often painful.

As it turned out this was the first of nineteen visits to see me over a period of some seven months.

Margaret appeared to look forward to these regular sessions and gained benefit and relief from talking about her life situation in addition to receiving actual hands-on healing. This illustrates another important point in regard to the healing process itself. Whilst most spiritual healers like myself are not trained counsellors, it is essential that the person coming for healing feels properly listened to. Unfortunately the hard-pressed doctor, whether GP or even specialist consultant, rarely has sufficient time to spare to enter into a more prolonged appointment and really create space to listen to what is in someone's heart and mind. However just these concerns may be very much related to the external physical symptoms of the illness or disease.

Through our regular healing sessions and the conversations that became part of them, it became very clear that Margaret had some significant and indeed long-standing emotional issues in her life. One of these issues concerned the premature and tragic death of a member of her family.

In spite of not being a counsellor I have found that in the context of a healing session and with the particular mood and atmosphere that accompanies it, i.e. essentially non-judgmental and receptive, it is often possible to offer appropriate words of consolation and comfort. Perhaps, like the healing energy itself, they are just 'given' to meet the needed situation. A healer is, after all, aware that he or she is being actively helped from a higher source to give the healing. More than once Margaret expressed what a relief it was for her to be able to share her problems and concerns.

Other issues for Margaret centred around the need for 'self-empowerment' and being able to live her own life, rather than being at the beck and call of her grown-up family. This again illustrates clearly the different levels of need which can co-exist within us. Not only can there be some obvious physical symptoms, and also emotional needs and unease, but spiritual needs in the area of one's self-experience, decision-making and self-determination can come to light as well. The acknowledgement and recognition of these diverse needs is all part and parcel of the holistic healing process.

As Margaret confided at our third healing session, she was also subject to depression and was taking medication to help relieve this.

The continuation of our regular sessions went from weeks into months and, little by little, Margaret said that she felt better in herself. She gained a more positive and optimistic outlook on her life and, in particular, towards herself. Her feelings of inadequacy and the burden of prolonged trauma and grief were lessened and lightened. With positive encouragement Margaret found the truth of the well-known proverb, 'Where there's a will there's a way.'

The healing invariably brought her a sense of peace and relaxation, at times almost verging on sleep, and the heartburn and painful left knee which had ostensibly been her reasons for seeking spiritual healing in the first place, were less problematic than they had been.

After a period of seven months when Margaret came for another healing session and I asked what I could do for her today, she replied that there didn't really seem anything more that was needed! We therefore agreed to stop and left it that she would contact me if any further healing was required. So far, and twelve months later, Margaret has not requested healing help which I choose to regard as good news!

Brenda

I had healing sessions with Brenda on and off over a period of two years. She also had problems which tended to undermine her health on different levels of her being. Physically and biologically there was a fairly long history of ill health, with some quite painful and specific symptoms involved. However, in addition, she had prolonged emotional issues which had actually overshadowed most of her life. She was then in her fifties. Brenda described herself as being very low emotionally and subject to anxiety and panic attacks. On the level of her individuality (the more inner, spiritual level), there were also considerable problems to do with self-esteem, empowerment, and decision-making. All in all, Brenda had a lot on her shoulders. In fact rather too much! She was fairly desperate for help and, generally speaking, had not enjoyed very positive experiences or support in relation to the various medical treatments which she had received over the years. Certainly these treatments had not cured her problems on the physical level nor anywhere else. Indeed it is likely that, emotionally and mentally, she felt worse rather than better!

Brenda, like Margaret before, needed space and time to tell her story and share her worries and concerns. However she also felt benefits, from the start, with the direct hands-on contact healing. Already when she came for her second healing session a week later Brenda reported: better sleep at night, no panic attacks, less pain in her lower back and left leg. She also felt better able to get on with things and said that she had a more positive outlook and greater inner peace.

Over the two year period in which Brenda received healing the frequency of her visits was generally rather irregular, sometimes with intervals of several weeks or more. She always felt better in herself after each healing session and, often, her physical aches and pains were also alleviated. However, the most outstanding benefit of the healings was seen in her increased ability to deal with the difficult situations which her life presented to her. These included her own health problems, but also wider issues to do with family and friends. Brenda found that she had stronger inner resources, and these enabled her to experience greater calmness and peace with herself. Instead of habitually knocking herself down, so to speak, she was now able to maintain a more positive and optimistic outlook. Although her physical problems, and there were several of them, had certainly not disappeared, she was now able to see them in a more measured perspective and, in that respect at least, she was in a better state of health and wellbeing than she had been when I had first met her.

As she has not contacted me for more than six months to request healing, I am again taking the attitude that, 'No news is good news,' and I wish her well.

Keith

Keith developed MS (multiple sclerosis) following a motorbike accident when he was 25 years old. About two years after this he went to a local Healing Centre to receive some hands-on spiritual healing.

He was taken to his first session in a wheelchair by his mother as Keith was unable to walk. He felt benefit from the healing and when he attended the Centre for the second session, a week later, he was able to walk slowly from the car park to his seat in the hall!

From thereon Keith was a regular participant at the weekly Healing Centre, which he attended for about nine years. It was here that I first met Keith during my last six months of healer training. Usually there were six or seven healers available to give healing to any members of the public that wished to receive it on the Wednesday evening when the Centre was open. The work was entirely voluntary and no charges were made, but any donations to help meet the costs of hiring the local hall, etc. were gratefully received. Invariably Keith chose me as his 'healer,' and we soon developed a good rapport. Since the Centre closed some two years ago, I have continued to visit Keith at his home, together with another healer friend of mine, on a fortnightly basis.

Although Keith walks with a decided limp, as his right leg is rather stiff due to his MS illness, he is well able to get about and he can drive a car. He always feels benefit from the healing sessions and, in particular, he experiences warmth flowing into his right leg. (When I first worked with Keith some three years ago this leg was markedly cold.)

Keith goes for an annual check-up to hospital in order to assess the state of his MS condition. Very recently when my fellow healer and I arrived at Keith's house for our regular session he was waiting at the door to meet us. He proceeded to usher us into the sitting room and with some enthusiasm told us about his visit to his local GP. His doctor had received a letter from the hospital where Keith goes for his MS check-ups, saying that they couldn't understand how he was keeping so well! Years ago it had been anticipated that his condition would worsen considerably. Keith himself has no doubts that it is spiritual healing which has helped him to keep his illness in remission.

Pat

I had been told by a friend of mine that her friend, Pat, was suffering from motor-neurone disease. I offered to visit to give her healing at home, and some days later Pat's husband phoned me to arrange a mutually convenient time.

After the first healing session I continued to visit Pat weekly over a period of some four months. From the outset her husband had said that the disease was degenerative and medically incurable. Nonetheless, Pat appreciated the regular healing and for a time I, and perhaps she also, was hopeful that the inexorable course of the illness might be thwarted or at least mitigated.

Unfortunately this was not to be, and after she had picked up a fluey virus in the late autumn her condition worsened fairly dramatically. Eventually she died, perhaps some six months since I had first met her. Pat lived life right to the end as fully as she was able to and, from her responses to the weekly healing sessions, I believe that she did obtain some benefit from these. We will, of course, never know if healing helped to give her precious extra time, but her cheerful and courageous disposition under the impact of such a chronic illness was very impressive to experience. Spiritual healing cannot always result in a cure, but it may well improve an individual's quality of life. I sincerely hope this was indeed the case for Pat.

Susan

A friend of mine, Susan, was having some problems with her right eye. She suspected blocked sinuses, and I therefore gave her some healing. Two days later I gave her further healing for what had now been diagnosed as 'shingles,' a painful nerve condition which if it affects the forehead near the eyes can lead to damaged sight if treatment comes too late. Her doctor therefore straight away prescribed an antiviral drug.

However to complement the medical treatment Susan

was more than pleased to receive daily healing sessions directed specifically over the troublesome, and at times very painful, area that was affected. Indeed her right eye had effectively closed-up.

During several of the early sessions when my hands were held close over her head, Susan said that she experienced a strong burning sensation, as if the nerve points in her scalp were being cauterised! (And perhaps they were.) After three sessions Susan felt that things were improving. Two sessions later her right eye was open normally and she had been up in the house all day. After two further sessions she felt well again.

Susan had no doubt that healing had helped her to make a quick recovery from her sudden, and quite unexpected, attack of shingles. It had been eight or nine days since the doctor's diagnosis and the start of treatment, both medical and complementary.

Jim

I was very surprised to see my friend Jim with his right foot in a plaster cast and walking with the aid of crutches. (This was the same Jim who had previously had trouble with a slipped disc in his back.) He had broken a bone in his ankle and also badly sprained the ligaments whilst playing football. I therefore offered him some spiritual healing, by contact, about three weeks before the cast was due to be removed. Although the doctor at the hospital had predicted that the bone would set alright, he said that the sprained ligaments could take months to recover and that Jim would need some physiotherapy.

I had three healing sessions with Jim whilst his foot was still firmly encased in plaster.

During the first session he experienced a lot of activity going on in his ankle, with some 'pulling sensations.' He also felt the touching of hands through the plaster, which took him by surprise. Five days later, in the second session, Jim once again experienced a 'pulling,' and also the stroking of my hand as I moved it down his leg and over his foot several times. At the end of the session Jim felt a lot of warmth and he said that his 'toes were glowing.' In the third session, a week later, there was no further 'pulling,' but a gentle warmth around the foot and also some aching when I stroked over the ankle. His own impression was that the foot was actually better.

When the three weeks were up Jim had the plaster cast removed and, at first, the ankle was somewhat swollen and tender. Another healing was given, and Jim felt the benefit of it. Less than a week later the foot was functioning normally and no further treatment was required, including no physiotherapy.

Unfortunately this was not the end of Jim's troubles. No sooner was his right foot successfully healed than he had a bad accident whilst tree-felling and broke his left leg! Moreover it was not a simple fracture as both the bones of the lower leg were broken near the ankle. Jim was taken by ambulance to hospital and, the following morning, an operation was performed to insert a metal rod into his lower leg to give support and to avert having to have a plaster cast on his leg for the next three months! The metal rod was secured by screws at the knee and near the ankle.

I visited Jim in hospital two days after his operation. He was lying in bed with his bandaged leg raised up and a morphine drip going into his arm to dull the pain. I asked him if he'd like some healing for his leg and he said that he would. I therefore first gained his doctor's permission to give him spiritual healing through the laying-on-of-hands.

Soon after beginning the healing Jim remarked that the

pain had gone. Later he also felt warmth flowing through his leg.

The next time I saw Jim to give him healing, just two days later, he was at home lying on his bed. He said that after I had left the hospital ward his doctor had come round and enquired how the healing had gone. Jim told him that he was now pain free and did not require any more morphine!

I believe there are good grounds to anticipate that with further healing sessions Jim's left leg will heal successfully and, perhaps, also quicker than is medically expected. We will have to wait and see as this is still 'work-in-progress' at the time of writing.

Addendum: I have since seen Jim several times for healing at his home. He is pleased with the good progress his leg is making, now only two weeks since the accident occurred, and he feels very confident that the bones will heal properly. He continues to be free of any pain.

Lucia

I will draw these examples of hands-on spiritual healing with people to a close with a short but amusing incident.

My teenage daughter is very keen on sports, particularly basketball and tennis, and she never misses any opportunity to get out onto the sports ground when in school.

One day recently when she returned from afternoon school she complained of a painful knee. I offered her some hands-on healing for her knee and, unlike her usual reaction to my well intentioned offers of help she didn't, on this occasion, decline. (Her usual reaction of decline for 'my' healing is quite in conformity with the attitude of her brothers and sister!)

After a short time with my hands on her knee 'the treatment' was concluded. About an hour later when I saw her rushing through the house I asked her how her knee was feeling. She replied that it was fine and, no doubt, it had just recovered spontaneously! After all healing can't really work, can it?

Not only people, but also animals, can sometimes benefit from spiritual healing. Two examples are given below. As it happens both are from the bovine family. Before giving healing I confirmed with the farmer that the animals were receiving the necessary veterinary treatment.

Horace

Horace was a young bullock who had had rather a rough ride! He had not been on his legs long before he was accidentally injured by his companions, i.e. trodden upon. He had received nasty injuries to his sides and was being treated by the vet.

When I saw him at the farm he was too weak to get back onto his legs. Only by means of a special hanging truss, to lift Horace up, could he spend some time on his legs. His situation was really quite critical.

I gave Horace hands-on healing over four or five sessions. He made a good recovery and, in time, was back on his feet. Since then he has grown up and is now an active breeding bull.

Nancy

Nancy was a mature dairy cow. Unfortunately however she suffered from clinical mastitis and was under treatment from the vet.

I gave Nancy some hands-on healing over a period of perhaps six weeks. Normally, after being milked, her milk would leave spots and clots on the filter paper through which it was poured. Each time Nancy received healing her milk passed more easily through the filter and the filter paper looked cleaner. Indeed sometimes the paper looked completely clear.

However in spite of this visible improvement, in between the healing sessions the signs of the mastitis returned again. Unfortunately healing was not able to overcome the condition; but neither could the vet's treatment!

Nonetheless Nancy continues to lead an active life and has meantime produced two calves.

With both Horace and Nancy the farmer felt sure that spiritual healing had had some beneficial results.

The critically minded and perhaps also the sceptical reader, whether interested lay person or health professional, may suspect that the anecdotal evidence given so far in this chapter for the 'Reality of Spiritual Healing' is quite possibly highly selective and perhaps not truly typical. What about any instances where healing has not yielded, or helped to yield, clearly beneficial results? To these quite reasonable sentiments I must answer that my selection of examples has been based on trying to present as wide a variety of ailments as I could, given the relatively short time that I have been offering hands-on healing, and that whilst healing is not always associated with a complete cure it has, almost invariably, given the individual at the receiving end a definite feeling of greater wellbeing and of inner peace and quiet. Never, to my knowledge, has it in any way exacerbated their health problem(s).

However it should be pointed out that it is sometimes possible for someone to go through what is often called a 'healing crisis,' when, in the course of the healing-process itself, they do actually get worse for a time before feeling better.

As the examples given above have illustrated, some ill conditions yielded very quickly whilst with others a gradual betterment was seen over the course of time.

The world famous spiritual healer, Harry Edwards, was convinced that the method of '*distant*' or '*absent*' healing was at least as effective as direct hands-on contact healing. This chapter would therefore not be complete without including a few examples of healing at a distance, though I would refer the reader to Edwards' own books which contain a large number of convincing examples of the efficacy of absent healing.

Absent healing, like hands-on spiritual healing, is actually a co-operative effort between healer, recipient, and the spiritual source(s) of healing energies. When a request for healing is made and, via the healer, passed on to the spiritual world, the healing flow can commence, rather in the manner of Christ's teaching, 'Ask and you will receive.'

My own practice of distant healing is also done in mindfulness of the work of the Harry Edwards Spiritual Healing Sanctuary at Burrows Lea in Surrey. More often than not those same people for whom I ask, in Christ's Name, for healing to be given at a distance, are also those for whom I write regularly for such healing help from 'The Sanctuary.' As a healer it is not a matter of gaining any personal credit or recognition for good results obtained — such credit is really quite unimportant. Edwards himself, in spite of being of help to many thousands of people, made it very clear that he could not heal anyone! As with other healers he was simply acting as a channel, or medium, for the flow of healing energies which were sent and directed from the spirit world in response to the request that had been made.

Ann

Ann has received distant healing again and again over a number of years. From time to time we speak on the telephone so that I can keep informed with how she and her family are getting on. She has four children still at school.

Ann has been chronically unwell for a long time now with a disease which has affected her nervous system but which, until very recently, had remained undiagnosed and unclear. It is now maintained that she has in fact MS (multiple sclerosis).

Over the past few years Ann has been referred to a number of medical specialists and she has therefore been subject to various tests and examinations. Their opinions and findings were however often rather divergent or else inconclusive. This left Ann feeling generally disaffected with medical opinions and treatments. She was put on a cocktail of drugs which included painkillers, such as morphine.

There is no doubt in her own mind and through personal experience that distant healing has helped and supported her more than other treatments. On those numerous occasions when we have linked-up at a specific time, Ann could often experience the direct benefit of the healing energies helping to bring her greater peace of mind and an alleviation of pain. Whilst the medical prognosis for her illness is not good, spiritual healing will continue to actively seek for the betterment of her health in every way that is possible. It has been, and still is, very impressive to see how positive, cheerful, and courageous Ann is in spite of her disabling physical state. She is a fighter!

John

John, a primary school age child, has some major health problems. Not least of these is his epilepsy. To make matters still worse John also then developed a particular type of epilepsy which caused abnormal brain activity during the night while he slept. The prognosis looked grim because the doctors did not know how to control the nocturnal brain disorder. It seemed inevitable that John would suffer from various irreparable losses of bodily function. Naturally John's family were very distressed about this situation.

At this point distant-healing help was requested for him. Some weeks later the doctors were happily surprised to see that the abnormal brain activity was actually mitigating. This had been beyond their expectations. It is still very early days yet and we must still see how John progresses.

George

George was getting on in years but he still liked to do some needed maintenance on his house until, that is, the unfortunate day came when he fell from his ladder and fractured the end of his spine. It was feared that the injury could be very serious. Indeed he might not be able to walk again.

However, luckily, the damage was not as bad as it could have been. George was nevertheless in a lot of pain and he was confined to bed. Soon after the accident distant-healing was requested on his behalf. George has made a good recovery, and in a shorter time than had been predicted. The acute pain gradually subsided and, by now, he is again able to drive his car and resume normal day-to-day life, though climbing ladders is definitely to be avoided!

Mark

Jill and Ken were devastated to learn that their eight-year-old son, Mark, was suffering from leukaemia. To make matters still worse the diagnosis was of acute myeloid leukaemia, which is rare in young children.

Naturally distant healing was started for Mark to *complement* his orthodox chemotherapy treatment. Being in hospital, over Christmas, and having to withstand the various procedures which his treatment required was very stressful and traumatic for young Mark and his parents. After two to three weeks of this, things were not looking at all good and when I spoke with Jill over the phone one evening, just before the New Year, it was clear that some very urgent help was needed. Mark had no energy, had lost a lot of weight, the spark had gone out of him and his mother, normally optimistic and hopeful, felt that time was running out. Under these circumstances and already around 10pm, I decided to contact the very experienced healers that I knew, Ray and Joan Branch. By telephone I explained the urgency of the situation and requested their help to send distant healing to Mark. This help was immediately promised, to join together with my own intercessions.

The next morning Jill rang to thank me for the change that had taken place in Mark. She said that he was a different child from yesterday. He had eaten; for the first time didn't complain of headaches; and nor did he speak of death or dying. The following day some of his drugs were reduced and he appeared to feel better in himself and had been awake all day. His father said that staff in the hospital were pleased with his progress. Eleven days after this improvement Mark was well enough to be allowed home, as it happened on his ninth birthday. This was a week earlier than had been planned for! He will have to return to hospital again for further treatment. Although Mark still has a very long way to go, and whilst spiritual healing can give no guarantees of cures, neither does it limit the good results that may be achieved.

Addendum: Since writing the above lines Mark has been

back in hospital again for nearly a week for another dose of chemotherapy. Jill informs me that he is doing 'brilliantly.' His doctors now place him in the 'middle' rate of risk whereas he was to begin with in the 'high' risk category. They also say that the cancer seems now to be in a state of remission.

Interestingly, when Jill told the doctor that Mark had also been receiving some distant healing, he said that a spiritual healer was working at the hospital and, perhaps, could be helpful!

Wouldn't it be wonderful if more hospitals were able to offer this particular complementary resource to their patients.

It would be quite possible to give further examples which are indicative of the reality of spiritual healing directed over a distance to strengthen and support the recovery, or at least betterment, of those who have suffered from accident or illness.

It should be emphasized that spiritual healing is not in any way in competition with orthodox medical practice or with the role of competent health professionals. Its sole aim is to seek for healing help in whatever way this may be possible for the greatest good of each individual. Spiritual healers would, I am sure, be more than happy to work more closely together with doctors and other health professionals, united in the common endeavour to serve the needs of their patients and to relieve the burden of suffering and sickness on whatever level it may be found, be it physical, emotional, mental, or spiritual. There is, I believe, ample accumulated and published empirical evidence from Harry Edwards and other very experienced healers to justify the claimed reality of spiritual healing.

6. Further Considerations

Very experienced spiritual healers have already published extensive accounts of their practice of spiritual healing, both in regards to hands-on contact healing and also absent or distant healing. There is however no one method or technique which is right for everyone. Therefore, either after the required healer training period (normally two years), or perhaps also during that time, new healers will need to discover what works best for them and for their patients. This is likely to be a journey of exploration and discovery.

As a comparatively new healer I would like in this chapter to share further some of my experiences so far, and also try to illuminate these by again turning to Rudolf Steiner's anthroposophy.

Whatever the outer way or procedure that is adopted in giving healing, whether it be simplicity itself as recommended by Harry Edwards, or something much more elaborate, all will be in vain if the inner attitudes and qualities of the healer are inappropriate. These inner attitudes include sympathy, compassion, and a loving non-judgmental viewpoint, combined with a will to do everything within one's power to be of service and assistance to the person in need of healing. Together with these attitudes the healer needs to develop a strong trust and confidence in the help that can, and will, flow through him or her from the spiritual world. No spiritual healer heals of himself or herself. The task is to be a willing, and fully conscious instrument, for the healing energies and forces.

Whilst no promises or guarantees of healing cures can, or

should, ever be given, at the same time no limits or restrictions should be prematurely imposed — after all, as the saying goes, 'With God all things are possible.' Healing is a process which usually takes time, patience, and perseverance; perhaps sometimes months or even years. One way or another it will involve changes; perhaps of outlook, attitude, lifestyle, relationships, prejudices, conceptions, etc. Each person is unique, each biography is special, and each illness, disorder, complaint, is also special for that particular person, even if it be nothing more than the common cold!

Some thirty years ago whilst a student at Emerson College in Sussex, I visited the Harry Edwards Spiritual Healing Sanctuary at Shere, in Surrey. I had been feeling very low and rather depressed. Things had not been working out at the College as I had initially hoped or planned. I was shown into the large country house and waited to see Harry Edwards (I had turned up impromptu, without prior appointment or warning). I did not ask for, or receive, any direct spiritual healing. What remains in my memory is Mr Edwards advising me not to take myself too seriously! I believe this was sound advice. At any event the year at Emerson, whilst challenging and calling for changes in myself in various ways, turned out very positively. Although healers, like Mr Edwards, are not usually trained counsellors, it can very well happen that words are spoken which can help to work wonders for the patient and which flow from that feeling of trust and confidence in the healing Spirit.

Essential for the healing process is the state of *'attunement'* to the patient and to the spiritual world. Like many other healers I enter into this state whilst standing behind the person who is seated for contact healing and, in lightly placing my hands on his or her shoulders, I inwardly become still and peaceful and ask that healing help will be given. It is of course an individual matter for each healer as to whom or to what they address themselves when asking for this help. In my case I always address myself to the Christ-Spirit, whom I consider to be ever-present with us, both within and without.

In the terminology of anthroposophy I would describe the state of attunement as one of bringing peace and quiet into my astral body and, at the same time, raising my awareness and intentionality to the healing task, to the reality of the spiritual world, and to my own higher self. It is something of a conscious crossing of a threshold, whereby one's own personal everyday concerns, worries, inhibitions, and doubts, can be put aside for the sake of being a willing channel for the Spirit. To do this needs of course perseverance and practice but, over time, confidence and assurance slowly grows. It may indeed eventually grow to be that 'supreme confidence' in the healing energies and healing guides which Harry Edwards both preached and practised in his life.

A very common experience both for healers and for those who are receiving healing is that of *warmth*, a warmth felt to be proceeding from the hands of the healer. I find that usually this warmth in my hands is quickly there when I attune to the person to be healed and to the Spirit. It was in fact many years ago that I first became aware of warmth sensations in my hands whilst sat quietly for the practice of meditation and concentration. Already then the question arose within me whether this warmth could somehow be used for healing. I put this very question to an elderly friend whom I knew to be a healer. Her reply was that if this was the case then it would, one day, become apparent — well, it did in my case more than twenty years later!

But where does this warmth come from, how does it

arise, what does it indicate? One experienced healer when asked, 'Why do people feel such heat in the healer's hands?' replied in all honesty 'No idea.'[1] Well I also have no definitive answer to this question but I believe that certain lectures given by Rudolf Steiner in 1920, can steer us in a helpful direction in our further understanding of spiritual healing. These three lectures, familiar to many anthroposophical doctors, are known as 'The Bridge' lectures, or, to give the full English title, *The Bridge between Universal Spirituality and the Physical Constitution of Man*.

Steiner there describes that the physical organism of the human being as it is conceived today (he was speaking in 1920 but it is likely that his remarks are just as relevant for our present time), is quite inadequate to describe the true state of affairs. This is because the human being consists not only of a solid/mineral part but has within him three other distinct organisms, composed of fluid, air, and warmth, and each of these finer physical organisms is connected with the respective supersensible member of man's fourfold being. As already pointed out in Chapter 2, the anthroposophical understanding of the human being identifies, in addition to the outwardly perceptible body, the etheric or life body, the astral or soul body, and the Ego or Spirit. In the Bridge lectures the four distinct elemental physical organisms are each related to the four bodily members so that we have:

Physical Constitution	**Bodily Members**
Solid organism	Physical body
Fluid organism	Etheric body
Aeriform organism	Astral body
Warmth organism	Ego

Steiner goes on to describe these relationships in some detail but his essential theme is to enable us to understand how, in the fourfold differentiated organization of man's physical constitution, we have also the connecting bridge to the cosmic spirituality. And it is, above all else, *the warmth* in man and in the cosmos which is the connecting link. Our own spiritual nature, the Ego, lives in this warmth. Only by a thorough study of the first two lectures can the reader grasp how Steiner explains these complex matters in detail. However, as he says:

> The warmth-organism is paramountly the field of the Ego… and … the Ego itself is that spirit-organization which imbues with its own forces the warmth that is within us …[2]

In the second lecture he then goes on to describe how enthusiasm for moral ideals such as, goodness, freedom, and love, which we carry within us, has a direct and stimulating effect upon our warmth-organism. This warmth-organism can then, in turn, stimulate in a very positive and healthy way the other organisms of air and fluid, right down to the level of the solid-mineral body of the human being. In other words a connecting bridge exists between what we carry in our inner soul-spiritual nature and our fourfold physical constitution.

> So we see that our whole constitution, beginning with the warmth-organism, is, in very fact, permeated with moral ideals.[3]

What then has all this to do with our understanding of the processes of spiritual healing?

When as spiritual healers we offer healing to those in

need, we act directly out of our moral idealism and out of our wish to be of service and help to our fellow human beings. Healing is nothing else but a vocation and a service. Furthermore, as spiritual healers, we act out of an awareness of the spiritual nature of the human being and the spirit sources of healing energies (whether we picture these sources as: God, the Divine, the Christ-Spirit, Angels, the Spirit-Guides, the Universal Energy Field, or whatever is most meaningful for us). This healing activity, fired by compassion and the will to do 'the good,' in which our own spiritual being (the Ego) plays its part, directly relates us to the universal sphere of warmth, to the warmth which facilitates and forms the essential linkage between Spirit and Matter. For this reason, I believe the sensation of warmth for both healer and patient is so often a striking and impressive part of the experience of spiritual healing. This warmth mediates the healing forces and energies right down to the solid physical body, from the levels of soul and spirit. To put all this in a very simple picture we could say that the warmth of the Spirit shines into us and works through us just as the rays of the outer Sun warm us externally.

In this connection I still vividly remember how when I visited a person who had recently, and suddenly, suffered a stroke and to whom I then offered some healing, I felt a strong sensation of warmth in the space near me. This happened on more than one occasion. I was already quite used to often experience a warmth around my head, but this was rather like an extensive mantle of warmth. Later, on reflection, I described this experience to myself as being comparable to sitting outside on a summer's day and being warmed through by the rays of the sun.

It is also interesting to see in the light of what has been said here, how Harry Edwards refers to the warmth sensation in spiritual healing:

> A common form of diagnosing the area of trouble is when the healer places his hand over the affected part, both the healer and the patient becoming aware of a strong heat emanating from the healer's hands and which appears to penetrate into the patient's body.'

He adds a few sentences later that:

> It is interesting to note that this heat is not clinical — that is, if a thermometer is placed between the healer's hand and the patient, there is no rise in the recorded temperature, though the heat sensation still exists... Study of this leads to the conclusion that the heat is not a physical heat at all. It does not arise from additional circulatory activity in the healer's body. It follows that the heat is *an expression of healing energy* directed from Spirit, through the healer.[4]

There seems to me to be a striking congruence here between Harry Edwards' observations, born out of years of healing practice, and the knowledge of the relationship between the human being and the spiritual universe given to us by Rudolf Steiner. In regard to warmth *per se* it is true to say that, on the basis of spiritual science, there is both a physical warmth and also a non-physical reality which Steiner designates as the Warmth Ether.

As with many healers the general procedure which I follow when giving contact healing is to work from the head downwards. First though I tune into the patient and the pure healing intentionality by standing behind him or her and resting my hands lightly on their shoulders whilst inwardly asking, in Christ's Name, for healing to be given. Then, from placing both my hands on the patient's head, to putting one hand near the top of the spine and the other near the base of the spine, to placing one hand over the centre of the chest and the other at the corresponding position on the back, and from there moving down to rest over the solar plexus area, once again with hands in front and behind. The procedure can then be to direct healing energies down the arms and legs, (each in turn), by placing one hand to the patient's shoulder whilst the other holds his/her hand, and, for the leg, to place one hand at the buttock and the other on the corresponding knee, perhaps then also proceeding from the knee to the foot. This procedure is not however invariable by any means. It depends on the situation and the patient's needs. As a healer I am also guided by my intuition as to 'where to go next' and also 'how long' to remain over any one area. I usually use this general healing method before focusing on any particular area of difficulty, for example, a sore or painful knee or elbow joint, a stomach problem, stiff neck, or whatever else it may be. As one of my original mentors, Dennis Fare, said, 'Treat the whole person first, and then go to the specific area if there is one.' (Sometimes when giving distant healing I will use a similar procedure whilst visualizing the patient sitting for healing in my room.)

A helpful healing image is to visualize that the healing energies are being enabled to flow freely through the patient's body, and that any 'blockages' to this energy flow are being overcome. The notion of blockages, restrictions, or congestions, in the flow of energy in the body is not very difficult to imagine. We are all familiar with such things as blocked noses or sinuses, restricted blood flow due to narrowed or clogged blood vessels, congestion in the lungs, stones in the kidneys, etc. etc. In the field of Curative Education Rudolf Steiner even speaks of a congestion of the astral and ego-organization in one or more organs of the body when he is explaining the real nature of epileptic seizures. Some clairvoyant healers have described how one or the other chakra can show blockages and congestions which prevent the healthy flow of vital energy throughout the chakra-system.[5] In short, we can well imagine that disruptions to the energy flow can sometimes occur on the physical, emotional, mental, and spiritual levels of our being for all manner of reasons; including the effects of fear, anxiety, insecurity, and stress. Some healers work with the 'human energy field' and, as part of this total field, also with specific chakra or energy centres. There are seven principal chakras, (though many lesser ones), positioned from the crown of the head downwards and mainly in alignment with the spine; the spine being considered as the central channel of energy flow between the various chakras. In addition to the crown chakra at the top of the head, there is a chakra in the area of the forehead, the throat, the heart, the solar plexus, the navel, and the base of the spine. In the literature on healing the correspondence between the endocrine glandular system and the seven main chakras is often cited, for example, as shown in the following diagram.

Chakras	**Location**	**Endocrine Glands**
Crown	Top of head	Pineal
Brow	Between eyebrows	Pituitary
Throat	Throat	Thyroid
Heart	Heart	Thymus
Solar Plexus	Base of sternum	Pancreas
Sacral	Navel	Gonads
Root	Base of spine	Adrenals

(However it should be noted that there are also some interesting differences in the healing literature about the chakras and the specific glands said to be associated with them.)

An awareness of and a working with the chakra-system is certainly an important feature for some experienced healers, such as Barbara Brennan, Michael Bradford, and Jack Angelo.

Rudolf Steiner was also very much aware of the main chakras and in his fundamental book on the path of inner spiritual development,[6] he refers to them as the 'lotus flowers.' However Steiner here describes these various chakras as the soul or astral organs for higher perceptions, whose careful and systematic development through the exercises he describes in his book can eventually lead to trained clairvoyance, as well as to other forms of supersensible perception and experience. In Steiner's approach to the development of the chakras for the purpose of attaining higher knowledge of worlds of soul and spirit, great emphasis is placed on the moral and ethical qualities which need to be developed and strengthened in the pupil who is following this path of inner training.

My reason for mentioning this aspect of Steiner's teaching is solely to point out that it appears that the chakras, as energy centres, can be approached at different levels. On the level of conscious inner spiritual development this is at the soul or astral level but for the purposes of *healing* it is the *etheric* level which is worked with and, as we have already seen, it is the etheric or life-body which is the real healer within us. The etheric body contains those vitalizing, life-giving forces which replenish, repair, and strengthen our physical body and its organ systems. Therefore the notion that spiritual healing can also be directed via the chakra system on the level of the etheric body, to help bring about a harmonious and balanced energy field may well have both validity and justification. I can only direct the reader to some of the interesting literature in which detailed accounts of working with the chakras in healing are to be found.[7]

Interestingly, Florin Lowndes in his book, *Enlivening the Chakra of the Heart*, also makes this important distinction:

> In the etheric body the chakras support the life-force and the energy necessary for maintaining the functioning and health of the physical body. Each chakra provides a supply of energy for a particular part of the body and its organs, including the endocrine glands, the nerve ganglia, etc. At this level the chakras regulate the life-processes — they are the spiritual organs of life, or life-organs.
>
> In the astral body the chakras support the development of the various aspects of consciousness — not only self-awareness but also higher, supersensible consciousness. The development of the chakras creates the basis for gaining knowledge of the higher, supersensible world and its beings. At this level the chakras are spiritual organs of spiritual perception.[8]

However, working consciously with the chakra system is definitely not a part of the healing performed in the tradition of Harry Edwards and as Ray Branch, a close healing colleague of Edwards, expressed it to me recently, his hallmark was to keep the healing procedure very simple and straightforward. For example, 'If someone had arthritis of the knee, Harry Edwards would not start at the head and work down — he would go straight to the affected joint.'

Whatever procedures, methods, or techniques individual healers or healer training organizations may choose to adopt, the practice of spiritual healing must be grounded on those inner qualities of sympathy, compassion, love, and service which were already cited at the beginning of this chapter. The healer serves as a conscious and willing instrument through which healing energies can flow to the one who comes to receive healing help and support. And perhaps, for many people, the more simply that this can be achieved, the better! As Bek and Pullar remark in their book, *The Seven Levels of Healing*:

> Remember that, on the highest levels, you, yourself, do nothing except raise the patient's consciousness in order to create possibilities. The less you do the better. The less of you there is, the more there will be of the highest levels. So tune into the highest levels and let them flow down.[9]

Finally, I have been asked quite often when someone has received healing through me, 'Does it tire you, does it use up your energy?' If this was a form of magnetic healing, such as Rudolf Steiner describes in the seventh lecture of his first course for young doctors, the answer to this question might well be 'yes.' As we have seen, in magnetic healing energy is transferred directly from the etheric body of the healer to the etheric body of the patient and, if this process is continued for a time, the healer will feel depleted and drained. However in spiritual healing the opposite experience occurs. Far from feeling tired, the healer can, like his or her patient, feel refreshed and vitalized. Spiritual healing therefore confers benefit on both parties, and this is the reason why I am not too keen on the use of the labels, 'healer' and 'patient.' For me healing is a shared, mutual, experience in which, by the grace of the Spirit, two human beings are allowed to participate in freedom and co-operation. Through this shared experience, whether it be by means of contact or distant healing, the greater awareness can dawn in us that because we are of an essential spiritual nature we can, therefore, receive real help by *spiritual* healing. However just because of the mutuality of spiritual healing its efficacy depends not only on the goodwill and competence of the healer, but also on the active receptivity and willingness of the patient to accept the healing energies. If there is a lack of receptivity the healing flow may be blocked or perhaps even rejected. In this respect it may not be irrelevant to ask the person who comes for healing if he or she really wants to be well and has the will to be healed. Some people, if the truth were known, would much prefer to hang on to their illnesses or disabilities, perhaps in order to gain the attention and care which this draws towards them. In the Gospel of St John, Chapter 5, before Christ-Jesus intervenes to help a man who had been crippled for thirty-eight years he asks him the question, 'Do you want to recover?' or, as it is rendered in a different translation, 'Is it your will to become whole?'

We might, so to speak, describe spiritual healing as a 'top-down' approach, rather than the usual 'bottom-up' approach via remedies and medicaments. Both directions become truly effective only if the etheric, health-giving body of the patient is stimulated and strengthened. Unfortunately it would appear that many of our modern antibiotics and drugs have the opposite tendency; namely to devitalize the person's own natural healing forces in the battle to destroy the viruses or bacteria which are often believed to be the root cause of illnesses and disease. Spiritual healing on the other hand, being both non-invasive and gentle and working out of a recognition of the whole person, invariably leads to a feeling of well-being, inner peace, and relaxation. Furthermore it is indeed likely that many physical illnesses have their real source on the level of the mind, soul, and emotions, and from there work down into the etheric and physical organisms. Therefore the experience in healing of being helped to come to peace, stillness, and relaxation, can be seen not only as a means of overcoming such psychosomatic disorders but also as an effective way of preventing such dis-eases taking hold in the first place!

7. Spirit Guides and Helpers

The notion that spiritual healers are simply channels for healing energies and that these energies derive from a spiritual, non-material, source is fundamental to the explanation and practice of spiritual healing, as is evident in the published literature on the subject.

However, equally fundamental is the conviction and/or experience amongst most, if not all, spiritual healers, that they are helped and guided in their practice by 'friends' across the threshold, i.e. beings acting from out of the spiritual world. These friends may be discarnate human souls, and/or more highly evolved beings belonging to the ranks of the spiritual hierarchies, that is angels, archangels, and so on. Some healers, such as Barbara Brennan, claim to be in conscious contact with their spirit healing guides. In turning to this particular aspect of healing, it is perhaps relevant to point out that although, historically, spiritual healing owes a certain debt to the rise of the spiritualist religion in respect of its legality and recognition, most healers are not in fact spiritualists.[1]

There is no doubt that Harry Edwards, who was one of the world's most experienced healers (and also a spiritualist), was entirely convinced of the active participation of spirit guides, whom he sometimes referred to as 'spirit doctors.' Indeed his own written explanations of spiritual healing, both direct contact healing as well as distant or absent healing, were founded on his unshakeable belief in the existence of these, usually, invisible guides. For example he writes:

> The healing guides alone are the administrators of the healing energies. Therefore, it is the guide who is able to make a correct diagnosis in order to know the character of the healing energies the patient needs. Thus the diagnosis is the responsibility of the guide and not the healer.[2]

He urged aspiring healers to have 'supreme confidence' in the help and direction which the guides could give from the side of Spirit. In the fascinating biography of Harry Edwards, his close colleague Ray Branch includes the following words of Edwards:

> For 15 years I did not know which particular guide was operating in my healing work. I was content with this position until, being repeatedly asked who were the healing guides working with me, I began to wish to know myself. In the past I had received numbers of descriptions of Spirit personalities who had been 'seen' working through me.[3]

Edwards therefore made efforts to find out the identities of his principal healing guides and through the co-operation of a well-known psychic artist, together also with confirmation from a medium, it was revealed that he was being guided by two eminent physicians. Namely, Louis Pasteur the great French scientist who discovered the cure for rabies, and Lord Lister the famous British surgeon and founder of antiseptic surgery. Pasteur died in 1895 and Lister in 1912. It was through being entirely convinced in the reality of his spirit guides that Edwards could have that 'supreme confidence' in his own healing work which he also encouraged others to gain in theirs.

This outspoken co-operative working with beings across

that threshold which, for our ordinary consciousness, separates the spiritual and physical planes of existence, is one of the most striking characteristics of spiritual healing. We can therefore ask the question, 'Does this alleged co-operation make any sense, is it really plausible, in the light of Steiner's anthroposophy?' I believe that the answer to this question is a resounding and unequivocal 'Yes!' Yes, that in many ways we can be and are assisted and supported both by discarnate human souls and also by spiritual beings, such as our own ever-present guardian angels, is confirmed again and again by Steiner in lectures which he gave in the first quarter of the twentieth century. Indeed all of us are helped much more than we ever realize by those across the threshold, whether we be healers or not. For example, in a lecture given by Rudolf Steiner in Nuremberg in 1918 he says:

> A great deal of what we undertake in life is really inspired into us by the Dead or by Beings of the higher Hierarchies, although we attribute it to ourselves, imagining that it comes from our own soul ... The knowledge that around us, like the very air we breathe, there is a spiritual world, the knowledge that the Dead are round about us, only we are not able to perceive them — this knowledge must be unfolded in Spiritual Science not as theory but permeating the soul as inner life.[4]

And towards the end of this same lecture he states that:

> There is nothing more important for life, even for material life, than the strong and sure realization of communion with the spiritual world.[5]

Steiner clearly indicated that there should in fact come about in future a far more conscious and active participation with those who have died. However it is also apparent in studying the various lecture cycles where he specifically deals with life between death and rebirth (the concept of 'reincarnation' is a central theme in anthroposophy), that particular care is needed in establishing a living dialogue with souls across the threshold. This is a realm where pitfalls and errors may easily occur owing to a lack of knowledge of the special characteristics of the way of communication between these two sides of life. In the Introduction to a recent book, *Staying Connected*, which contains selected talks and meditations by Rudolf Steiner, we read that:

> Those who have passed through the gates of death want to work with us on the physical world. This working together only appears to be a physical collaboration, for everything physical is only an outer expression of spirit. Materialism has alienated human beings from the world of the dead. Spiritual science must help us to make friends again with that world ... We are not just human beings, we are also tools — instruments for the spirits who have passed through the gate of death.[6]

Naturally any short quotations made from the lectures of Rudolf Steiner should, whenever possible, be also reviewed in their proper context. Nonetheless what has been included here makes it perfectly clear that Steiner anticipated a much more active working together between people who are at present incarnated on the earth and those who are discarnate. Therefore the conviction which many spiritual healers have that there *are* friends in the spirit world who actively help and support them in their healing tasks seems not only possible, but very likely to be the reality.

Harry Edwards thought it probable that, for example,

dedicated doctors who had devoted their lives on earth to helping the sick and suffering would, after death, also wish to continue this healing work if it were possible for them to do so. That such possibilities exist after death is, I believe, supported by Steiner's remarks that:

> Everything we are able to accomplish on earth with devotion, with love for the task at hand so that we are completely involved in what we do and realise that what we do is worthy of man, contributes to making us after death servants of the spiritual beings of the higher hierarchies who send healing, constructive forces from the spiritual into the physical world.[7]

When we also remind ourselves that the qualities of compassion, love, and a strong will to help and heal, must be the hallmarks of all genuine healers, then it is not at all difficult to imagine that friends across the threshold will feel called upon to collaborate in an active and justified way. Indeed love and warmth of heart and feeling, provides the very soil in which our relationships with those who have died can continue to grow and develop. Love is that which forms the bridge between all levels and planes of existence.

The anthroposophical physician, Dr Rita Leroi, in her book, *Illness and Healing in the context of Cosmic Evolution*, points out, in reference to the meditative exercises which Rudolf Steiner recommended in his lecture course for young doctors, that:

> Regularly carried out, such exercises will create a relationship between our astral bodies and the healing spirits whom we encounter in the periphery during the night. In the morning, we may then experience how

> the urge to give help grows stronger all the time, thanks to these night-time encounters.[8]

Her remarks, no doubt based on long experience, can also lend further weight to the conviction of many spiritual healers that their efforts to offer help do indeed receive both guidance and support from the spheres of Spirit. There are those who are both willing and able to help us to heal! Indeed the whole field of healing has long been associated with the influence of the archangel Raphael and also with the winged messenger of the gods, Hermes or Mercury. The Mercury Staff, or caduceus, is well known as an emblem of the medical profession.

Nonetheless Rudolf Steiner did warn about certain real dangers and pitfalls in regard to 'mediumship' and presumed communication with the world of the dead, and it is good to be aware of these when reading some interesting modern accounts of mediumship.[9]

Steiner describes, for example, how it can happen that after death the lower part of a person's astral body may continue to live on in the soul world while the actual spiritual individuality (the Ego), of the person has progressed to higher planes of existence.

> This (astral) corpse continues to hover about in astral space and may be a source of many dangerous influences.
>
> This too is a body which can manifest in spiritualistic séances. It often survives for a long time, and may come to speak through a medium. People then come to believe that it is the dead man speaking, when it is only his astral corpse. The corpse retains its lower impulses and habits in a kind of husk; it can even answer questions and give information, and can

> speak with as much sense as the 'lower man' used to display. All sorts of confusions may then arise ...[10]

Clearly then we need to be aware that we cannot take so-called communications and messages from the dead simply at face value. There is a need for knowledge, discrimination, good common sense, and a certain healthy feeling for truth in these matters. Nonetheless genuine communications with a deceased person's spiritual individuality can occur,[11] and Steiner was also very clear that a helpful and *conscious* co-operation could certainly be established between us and friends on the other side of life. When we bear in mind that a main task of spiritual healing may well be to help awaken more and more people to the reality of the Spirit, then the following observation by Steiner, made in 1910, is also very relevant.

> Because there are so many people completely in the dark, who have woven so much darkness into themselves that they wish to know nothing about the spiritual world, there are, on the other hand, among the dead many who have the impulse to work into the physical world.[12]

In this respect it is particularly interesting to read the impressive accounts (Fuller 1975, Solomon 1997) of the work of two outstanding psychic surgeons, namely the Brazilian José Arigo (1918–71) and the Englishman Stephen Turoff. Both these men working in a state of trance, became the mediums or instruments for whole teams of Spirit doctors working together with their main guides. Arigo, known as 'the surgeon of the rusty knife,' was possessed by the guiding spirit of a deceased German doctor, Dr Fritz, who then performed countless operations and wrote complex prescriptions.

Similarly Stephen Turoff is used by a Dr Kahn, interestingly also of German descent. Many thousands of patients have it appears benefited from the work of these dedicated psychic surgeons, and no doubt their patients' beliefs in a supersensible world have also been stirred, or perhaps jolted, to life!

(For clarity it should however be noted that 'psychic surgery' is not included in the official definition of 'spiritual healing' given in the published Standards of UK Healers.)

An interesting slant on the question of spirit guides is given by Bek and Pullar when they write,

> It is best wherever possible for the healer to tune into his own higher self. It can be reassuring to have one or two guides around but they should be training us to stand on our own two feet, teaching us to heal on our own. It is a common mistake to think that the guide is hovering about somewhere outside and so sit back, relying on him, when with enough determination and imagination we could get on with the healing by ourselves.[13]

Clearly this viewpoint seems very different from that of Harry Edwards which was cited at the beginning of this chapter. The issue here is the degree of dependancy involved; not the reality of guides *per se*.

Nonetheless I must admit that I do find the psychic portraits of three of my own alleged guides quite reassuring!

It is likely that only a small number of spiritual healers believe themselves to be clearly aware of the specific identity of their spirit guides and helpers. However this may be, I think it is of immeasurably greater importance for us, as healers, to feel confident that we are indeed supported in our efforts by 'friends' across the threshold, both human and hierarchical, who are working for mankind's true benefit and well-being. If we take care to set ourselves high ethical standards and are genuine and sincere in our motives and intentions to heal and to serve the needs of those who are sick and suffering, then I believe it is reasonable to assume that we will also receive whatever protection may be required to guard against any possible negative influences. Once again, the level of consciousness we exercise as spiritual healers is of no small importance, and this heightened awareness should be developed during the period of training. We do after all have to accept full responsibility for whatever we ourselves do.

8. Competence and Training

In December 2000, *The Alliance Review*, the magazine of the British Alliance of Healing Associations (BAHA), referred to a report by Exeter University revealing that there were some 15,424 healers in the UK, but with only sixty of these working in the NHS.* In an earlier issue of the same magazine (December 1999), the BAHA Chairman's Report made reference to a figure of some 20,000 healers in the UK.

Also in 1999, researchers at the Centre for Complementary Health Studies at Exeter University were commissioned by the Department of Health to conduct a study of the professional organization of Complementary and Alternative Medicine (CAM) bodies in the United Kingdom. The study results suggested that there were approximately 50,000 CAM practitioners in the UK. Therefore the number of healers, approximately between 15,000–20,000, represents a considerable proportion of the total number of estimated CAM practitioners.

Spiritual healers are members of a range of larger or smaller healing associations in the UK. According to its publications leaflet, the National Federation of Spiritual Healers (NFSH), founded in 1954, is acknowledged to be the principal organization specifically for spiritual healing in the UK, with more than 6000 members. In comparison, the World Federation of Healing (WFH), founded in 1977, is a body whose membership is open to qualified practitioners of any

* Naturally many of the figures included in this chapter will be subject to ongoing revision and update.

discipline of healing, including registered medical practitioners. It has currently nearly 1000 members. The Spiritualists National Union (SNU) has over 3000 members.

However, the great majority of the 'local' county and other associations in the UK are comparatively small in size, such as, for example, the Bristol District Association of Healers, which covers Bristol and the adjoining counties of Wiltshire, Somerset, Monmouthshire and Gloucestershire and has, at present, just one hundred members.

Given the number of small associations dotted around the country, already more than twenty years ago, there was clearly a need for some sort of overall umbrella organization which could represent their common interests. Thus it was that in 1977, the British Alliance of Healing Associations, was formed. Today the Alliance comprises around 30 autonomous healing associations with a total combined membership of approximately 3500.

Another and wider umbrella organization was later also formed in addition to BAHA. This was known as the Confederation of Healing Organizations, or CHO for short. In common with all the larger and smaller affiliated groupings it is a registered charity and, recently, forms a national confederation of sixteen independent Healing Associations (including BAHA, NFSH, WFH, etc.), representing some 12,000 healers. CHO's prime objective was to establish healing as a standard therapy for the National Health Service as well as for private medicine. To this end, and during the 1980s and 1990s, CHO demonstrated a coherent approach to the delivery of non-conventional therapy in a respectable way that merited serious consideration. So that, for example, in 1986 while the BMA's (British Medical Association's) Report on Alternative Medicine was apparently somewhat hostile to every therapy, it noted with surprise CHO's willingness to subject spiritual healing to trials by independent medical scientists. In 1991, the Chairman of CHO was invited to speak at Westminster to the Parliamentary Group for Alternative and Complementary Medicine on 'Respectable Healing.'

By 1993 the Department of Health confirmed to CHO that the Government's 'Patient's Charter' covered requests by patients in NHS hospitals to see a healer. Throughout the 1990s CHO, as the lead body for healing in the UK, exercised on behalf of its member organizations a very active influence for the greater recognition and acceptance of healing within the mainstream of healthcare attitudes, issues, and policies, both nationally and, more recently, also in the European Parliament. Spiritual healing is legal in the UK, since 1951, and NHS doctors can refer patients to qualified healers. Unfortunately this recognition and legality is not yet enjoyed across all the countries of Europe.

About three years ago the European Confederation of Healing Organizations, ECHO, was formed and has at present approximately 26,050 members; 3400 of them in Germany, 2000 in Romania, 250 in Denmark, 200 in Norway, 200 in Austria, and around 20,000 in the United Kingdom.

Of course a vital core issue in respect of the quality of the contribution which spiritual healing has to offer in the mainstream of modern healthcare, is that of *competence and training*. It has to be evident and transparent to members of the public and to other healthcare professionals, that spiritual healers have indeed acquired the necessary degrees of proficiency and competence. This requires that an approved course of training is in place. In other words, there must be definitive safeguards which regulate, monitor, and give assurance of high quality 'good practice.'

For many years both CHO and BAHA as the two

umbrella organizations for healing in the UK have already had clear mandatory Codes of Conduct in place, with equally clear Complaints and Disciplinary procedures. All associations affiliated to these two bodies have likewise had their own Codes and Constitutions which have conformed to the high ethical Standards set by CHO and BAHA. For example, included in these requirements is the condition that 'Healers should only heal in a conscious state of attunement. Trance conditions are neither recognized in law nor covered by CHO's insurance.' All probationer and trainee healers as well as full-healer members must agree to abide by these conditions and requirements, and likewise all members are insured for direct hands-on spiritual healing.

However all these conditions and requirements were brought into a much higher profile recently through the House of Lords Inquiry by the Select Committee appointed to consider Science and Technology, and which was ordered to report on *Complementary and Alternative Medicine*. The final treatise, the Sixth Report, published on 21 November 2000, is some 172 pages long and the Summary, which precedes the nine chapters, begins by saying that:

> 1. The use of complementary and alternative medicine (CAM) is widespread and increasing across the developed world. This raises significant issues of public health policy such as whether good structures of regulation to protect the public are in place; whether an evidence base has been accumulated and research is being carried out; whether the practitioner's training is adequate and what the prospects are for NHS provision of these treatments. It was the need to consider these issues that prompted this Inquiry.

In short, the Report makes it very clear that complementary and alternative medicine, therapies, and treatments, must either provide their own rigorous means of voluntary self-regulation, quality-assurance, and competence, or else the Government would have to do it for them by imposition and statute in order to protect the public. The Report ends with the statement that,

> 9.46 We recommend that only those CAM therapies which are statutorily regulated, or have a powerful mechanism of voluntary self-regulation, should be made available, by reference from doctors and other healthcare professionals working in primary, secondary or tertiary care, on the NHS.

The Government's response to the House of Lords Select Committee was to strongly encourage the regulating bodies within each therapy, to unite to form a single body for each profession. The single body which was subsequently formed to serve this function for spiritual healers in the United Kingdom is known as UK HEALERS.

All healing organizations that collaborate under the name UK HEALERS continue to retain their independence and autonomy but are working towards Common Minimum Standards of practice to ensure that the public can visit their spiritual healer with confidence and trust. The healer members of all organizations that meet the UK HEALERS standards, must follow a Code of Practice which meets the high levels of professionalism in healing and complementary therapy expected by the public throughout the UK. The aim is that they will have official recognition for meeting these standards. The work of UK HEALERS is encouraged and supported by the Prince of Wales Foundation for Integrated Health. UK HEALERS is, therefore, the new lead body in healing matters and no longer CHO.

At the time of writing this chapter some forty healing organizations are co-operating with UK HEALERS and these include CHO, BAHA, NFSH, WFH, and SNU. Through the wide representation, discussion, and dialogue which has taken place during the past three years on the various drafts towards the final form of the Minimum Standards for Training and Development, it is now hoped that within a quite short time UK HEALERS will have achieved the registration and recognition by the Government that is required of all voluntary, self-regulatory, CAM bodies. From this a national Register of Approved Healers is likely to come into being in the near future.

On the basis of what knowingly has to be included in the Minimum Standards a very great deal of hard work has already been done in providing full healers and trainees with the required contents and material. For example, the British Alliance of Healing Associations published in 2002 its *Training Guide for Tutors and Probationers*, and in January 2003 the World Federation of Healing also published its own very comprehensive and detailed *Training Manual*.

Whilst it is not possible in the scope of this book to describe in any detail the actual contents of the above mentioned *Training Guide* and *Manual*, common topics which have to be covered in the trainee's development as a spiritual healer over the two year probationary period include:

- Background to Healing
- The Role of the Healer
- Explaining Healing to a New Patient
- Healing Procedure
- Distant Healing

- Healing of Animals
- Basic Listening and Counselling Skills
- Spiritual Attunement, Meditation, and Psychic Protection
- Anatomy and Physiology
- First Aid Awareness
- The Code of Conduct
- Articles of Constitution
- Healing and the Law
- Confidentiality
- Relationship to Medical Profession
- Record Keeping, Disclaimers, and Data Protection Act
- Complaints and Disciplinary Procedures
- Setting up a Healing Centre

This topic list is by no means exhaustive and, for example, in the *World Federation of Healing Manual* there are some 27 topic/chapters and, corresponding to these, also 27 detailed Lesson Plans designed to cover thoroughly the Aims and Objectives of Healer Training.

Each healing organization needs to have a number of experienced full healer members who are able and willing to implement the training programme with trainees, both in terms of theory and practice. That is to say there are designated Healer Trainers. Indeed some organizations such as the National Federation of Spiritual Healers have already had their own Trainers for many years in order to implement their clearly structured residential and non-residential Healer Training Courses.

While the actual methods and degrees of Assessment of trainees' development as healers over the two-year probationary period may vary somewhat from organization to organization, clearly the basic requirements needed to meet the Minimum Standards for Training and Development of UK HEALERS, and the Government, must be fulfilled by all the healing associations who are following the policy of voluntary self-regulation.

Although the UK HEALERS guidelines on the area of trainee assessment are not yet finalized, it is anticipated that some form of external verification of the standards achieved by the trainee will also be necessary.

There will of course be an ongoing assessment process especially in regard to the actual practice of healing because however much theory or study a trainee may undertake in order to meet, or to exceed, the Minimum Standards, it is of course the regular practice under the supervision of a qualified healer that is of the greatest importance. Not least, to encourage the trainee's own self-development, confidence, and sensitivities, as a healer.

In this regard I consider myself to have been extremely fortunate when, at the age of fifty-one, I began my training in spiritual healing at the Dennis Fare Healing Centre in Bristol. Mr Fare not only had more than fifty years experience as a spiritual healer but was also a past President of the National Federation of Spiritual Healers (succeeding Harry Edwards), and additionally, a founder member and President of the World Federation of Healing. Indeed the vision of a multi-national World Federation encompassing all healing therapies, including spiritual healing, was actually Dennis Fare's brainchild. Dennis, together with his wife Doreen who herself has more than thirty years of healing experience behind her, were my Mentors for the first year of training. Without their confidence in my own developing abilities to channel the healing-energies it would be highly unlikely that I would be writing this book today or that I would ever have achieved full-healer status! It can be, and certainly was in my case, daunting to place one's hands, for the purpose of giving healing, on to a complete stranger who is in very real need of such help. In my experience it is the gradual gaining of confidence in oneself and trust in the healing forces and those in the spiritual world who help to direct and guide them, that is the make or break of a potential healer! This is a point I wish to emphasize also for the benefit of others because the steady attainment of confidence, together of course with deepened compassion and a genuine will to help and to heal, is an essential characteristic of a competent healer.

This confidence does not of course mean falling into the trap of promising the patient that he or she will be 'cured' by your intervention. Indeed it is clearly stated in the Code of Conduct that healers should not claim the ability to cure or heal anyone. Rather it is a confidence that grows through the conviction that the request for help for the patient, when directed to the source of healing, will be answered in every way that is possible at that particular time and under the conditions which prevail. To ask for 'the greatest good' to come about for the benefit of one's patient is not to presume to know beforehand exactly how this can manifest or be fulfilled! Both confidence and also a certain humility are required here.

The inner development of the healer through the practice of spiritual attunement and learning to meditate is an essential part of the two-year probationary period and is clearly incorporated into the Training Programme. Such inner development, whether it has recourse to simple prayer or meditation, will be an ongoing necessity for the qualified healer. Belonging to this inner work will be the awareness of how to protect oneself against any possible negative influences, thoughts, or emotions.

As was mentioned in the introduction to this book some healers are certainly clairvoyant to a degree and may also have other psychic abilities and sensitivities. It is however important to be clear about one's intentions and task when acting as a spiritual healer and I feel strongly that there should, for example, be a very clear separation made between the giving of healing and any form of mediumship and/or clairvoyance. Mediums have a specific role to offer to those who choose to come to them, and healers have quite another.

Each healing act is an individual and unique situation and challenge. Inwardly and outwardly it can, and perhaps always should, have something of the quality of a sacramental service. The healer, and perhaps the patient, having an awareness of a divine and spiritual influence being called upon can create a sacred space in which the Good may be done. Healing does indeed require a very high standard of ethics and responsibility — though a touch of humour is often also of real benefit! It is clearly essential that members of the public who turn to spiritual healers for help and support, are confident that the best level of 'good practice' will be offered to them. The work of UK HEALERS is aimed precisely to give all of us this quality assurance for spiritual healing and it is heartening that the 'Standards' upheld by UK HEALERS have been published in 2003 in a fifty-page booklet, after a work-in-progress of some four years.

From now on healing organizations which meet, or exceed, the Minimum Standards set by UK HEALERS will qualify as being 'accredited,' and their approved healer members will gain 'registered healer' status. Individual healers will not therefore be accredited by UK HEALERS directly, but always via their own healing organization.

The Standards booklet is divided into eight clear sections under the following headings:

- Introduction — Objects, Standards & Definitions
- Membership
- Training

8. Competence and Training

- Code of Conduct
- Healing and the Law
- Assessment
- Complaints
- Disciplinary Procedures

Whilst it is true to say that healing organizations as affiliated members of BAHA and CHO have had such matters in hand for many years, nonetheless in presenting the contents for required Minimum Standards now in such a clear, comprehensive, and transparent way, UK HEALERS should indeed be able to fulfil the Government's demand for a competent single regulatory body within the United Kingdom for the self-regulation of spiritual healers. This acceptance will then mark a further major step forward in the recognition of spiritual healing as a valued and holistic complementary healthcare resource. A resource which can moreover help to connect us again with our own essential spiritual nature.

Conclusion

As was pointed out in the Introduction my purpose in writing this book was not simply to add to the already available and very detailed literature on the theme of spiritual healing, but rather research this form of healing in the light of Rudolf Steiner's spiritual science or anthroposophy. To this end I have referred to specific remarks by Steiner in which he clearly acknowledges the reality of 'the laying-on-of-hands,' of 'psychic' and so-called 'magnetic' healing. Naturally it would be of great interest to know what Rudolf Steiner would say today if he were asked, specifically, about the nature of *spiritual* healing at it is now practised by many healers. Is the great wave of interest in alternative and complementary forms of healthcare, yet another symptom of that growing awareness of a spiritual and soul dimension to our human nature and, at the same time, a clear disaffection with what seems to be the increasingly technological and materialistic viewpoint of so much of modern medicine and science?[1]

While the practice of healing through the laying-on-of-hands goes back well before the time of Christ, when human beings lived in a very different world than we do now and also had a very different consciousness and constitution,[2] it is possible nowadays to develop such healing for the benefit of others in a fully conscious and free way. This, I think, is what aspiring healers can learn to do and that therefore spiritual healing is indeed a reality that can be made available to those who choose to ask for it.

In the book by Bernard Nesfield-Cookson, entitled, *Rudolf Steiner's Vision of Love*, he quotes the following passage from Steiner:

> All those acts of healing dependent upon what we may call a 'soul-spiritual healing process' must have the characteristic that selfless love is part of the process. In some form or other all soul-spiritual healing depends on a stream of love — which we pour into another person like a balsam. All that we do in this sphere must be founded in love.[3]

Therefore to the oft-asked question, 'What actually *are* the healing energies?' I believe we can reply, 'In essence, and at the highest level, they are nothing else but the energy and power of unconditional and universal Love.' This is a really concrete power in the world. If we then enquire, But what is the character of this universal Love? we could well meditate on the following words of St Paul in his First letter to the Corinthians:

> Love is patient; love is kind and envies no one.
> Love is never boastful, nor conceited, nor rude;
> never selfish, not quick to take offence.
> Love keeps no score of wrongs; does not gloat over
> other men's sins, but delights in the Truth.
> There is nothing love cannot face; there is no limit
> to its faith, its hope, and its endurance.[4]

These wonderful yet very challenging words of St Paul can help to give us that enthusiasm, that supreme confidence in the healing Spirit, which can lead us to experience *the reality of Spiritual Healing* in our modern and, unfortunately, still often very troubled world. And if we do our humble best to realize these words again and again in our daily life with others, we may perhaps also then begin to experience something of that ever-present spiritual source of healing which St Paul acknowledged consciously in himself with the words: *Not I, but Christ in me.*

Appendix 1
Some Healing Methods

The reader may well be aware that spiritual healing through the laying-on-of-hands, is not the only form of healing method in which the hands are said to be used for the transmission of healing energies or forces.

Dr Richard Gerber, in Chapter 10 of his comprehensive book, *Vibrational Medicine for the 21st Century — a Complete Guide to Energy Healing and Spiritual Transformation*, surveys the variety of hands-on healing methods. He introduces his chapter by pointing out that:

> Known by a variety of names — including bio-energy healing, psychic healing, paranormal healing, spiritual healing, Therapeutic Touch, Reiki, Johrei, Mari-el, SHEN therapy, pranic healing, and a bevy of other terms — laying-on-of-hands healing is perhaps the oldest form of vibrational therapy used today.[1]

Therefore the interesting, and important, question arises, 'How does spiritual healing *per se* differ, if indeed it does, from say reiki, therapeutic touch, etc.?' Now it has clearly not been the aim of the present book to explore this particular question. To do so properly would require not only a thorough review of the outer techniques and methods of these differently named healing disciplines but also, and I think more importantly, insight into their various philosophical and spiritual backgrounds. My own examination of spiritual healing in the light of Steiner's anthroposophy has laid special emphasis on the role of the unconditional and universal forces of Love which flow from the Christ-Impulse as it is described, centrally, in Rudolf Steiner's teachings.

However as both reiki and therapeutic touch are two types of healing that are becoming increasingly well known, it is perhaps justified to say just a little about them here.

Reiki

Reiki is a healing system that has its roots in the Far East, in Japan. The founder of this system was Dr Mikao Usui who was born in Japan in 1865 and sent as a very young child to a monastery school run by Tendai Buddhist monks. It appears that he studied martial arts and also learned meditation and healing. Seemingly Dr Usui had many different jobs including being a government officer and a journalist. He also studied other forms of Buddhism and, in his fifties, began training in Zen Buddhism. He underwent a strict spiritual discipline which enabled him to become enlightened and to acquire access to healing energy (reiki), and also to pass the ability to receive the reiki onto others.

In 1922 he opened his first clinic in Tokyo where he practised and taught reiki. It appears that Dr Usui's teaching was as much about spiritual awakening as healing, and in his teachings an emphasis was placed on using reiki for *self-healing*, as well as following certain definite precepts in one's daily life. In a sense reiki becomes, it seems, a way of life.

In the late 1930s reiki was introduced into the West by a young woman from Hawaii called Hawayo Takata, who travelled widely in the USA and in Canada. She also taught people how to use reiki for themselves. However since Mrs Takata's death, in 1980, there have developed more than thirty varieties of reiki that are practised in the West! (See

Quest, 2002, Chapter 20, for a brief description of these different types of reiki.)

The word reiki means Universal Life Force. This Life Force is said to be everywhere and yet in order to have access to this creative energy for self-healing and healing others Dr Usui created a process of initiation. According to one well accredited reiki master and teacher, initiation for accessing reiki:

> Is the vital key that separates Reiki's power and simplicity from other forms of healing and therapy.[2]

There are in fact three levels, or degrees, of reiki training, and 'First Degree' involves four initiations or attunements. Unlike spiritual healing where the healer attunes himself or herself in order to channel the healing energy, in reiki training the student is attuned by the Master. You cannot self-attune. However once the initiations have taken place the student has, it seems, gained life-long access to this Universal Life Force.

> The moment of initiation brings about union with Reiki — union with the Divine — and needs respect. It is a ritual of invocation and direction of Divine Light, a holy act of purification. The initiation in itself will transform as it changes the essential vibrational frequency of the student.
>
> ... Once the full initiation has taken place, this alignment remains eternally.[3]

'Second Degree' reiki also has an initiation process in the course of which certain special symbols are taught and also mantras are given. The 'Third Degree' is then the Master level. How the initiations are actually performed is not fully revealed to the student. However one reiki Master has, controversially, published details of this, including the special symbols and mantras which are used.[4]

The actual procedure and form for self-healing and for healing others in reiki practice is very methodical, with the hands being placed in definite sequential positions on the body. Indeed this Form element, to which the initiations are an essential part, is a main feature of reiki practice. It is stressed that self-treatment is the most important aspect of reiki. This is therefore also another significant difference between reiki and spiritual healing, since the latter is clearly directed to the service and the healing of others rather than oneself. Sandi Leir-Suffrey[5] points out that different reiki Masters deal very differently with the training of students in terms of the intervals of time between being initiated into the First, Second and Third Degrees. In this regard she urges caution to not rush forward in haste, but rather to allow sufficient time to gain practice and experience and, therefore, to also choose one's Master carefully!

It is said that reiki heals on the physical, mental, emotional and spiritual levels. Distant healing methods are also taught, though only at Second Degree level.

Finally it should be mentioned that in reiki practice it is usual to charge fees, whereas spiritual healing is generally offered on the basis of free-will donations only. However it is true that the comparatively small number of full-time, professional spiritual healers will also need to charge for their services.

Therapeutic Touch

Whereas reiki has its origins in the Far East, therapeutic touch has emerged in the West, in the USA. It has been taught to thousands of health professionals and is available at hundreds of hospitals and teaching centres worldwide. In the appendices to Dolores Krieger's book,[6] the names and addresses of Health Facilities where therapeutic touch is practised and also Schools, mainly of Nursing, where it is taught are listed. The great majority of all these places are situated in the USA or Canada.

According to Janet Macrae, an experienced therapeutic touch practitioner:

> Therapeutic touch has been derived from the ancient practice of the laying-on of hands. It is based on the fundamental assumption that there is a universal life energy that sustains all living organisms.[7]

The modern introduction of this form of healing in the USA was due principally to Dora Kunz, a gifted therapist and clairvoyant with whom Dr Dolores Krieger, a professor of nursing, collaborated in the 1970s. It was Krieger who coined the name therapeutic touch. Clinical scientific experiments were successfully conducted to show that therapeutic touch worked.

The principle underlying the practice of therapeutic touch is the bringing into balance and harmony of the energy field of the patient. It involves the use of the practitioner's own energy field as an instrument to help rebalance the patient's field which may have become obstructed, congested, blocked and disordered by disease. Interestingly, in therapeutic touch practice the therapist's hands are used several inches away from the patient's skin and clothing and not, usually, in any direct touch contact.

The practitioner must learn how to inwardly centre him or herself in order to be a conduit, or channel, for universal life energy to be directed to the patient. This inner condition, or conscious state of 'centred consciousness,' is said to be the source from which therapeutic touch gains its power.

It is therefore crucial to the whole process and is actually of much greater importance than the outer techniques that may be employed. The therapeutic touch therapist has to learn to cultivate that centre of peace and serenity within the heart region, and to know this as an attribute of the true self.

As Krieger expresses it:

> The point of entry into the Therapeutic Touch process is the act of centering. The therapist remains on-center even while proceeding with other phases of the Therapeutic Touch process: the assessment, rebalancing and reassessment of the healee's vital-energy field. The Therapeutic Touch therapist acts as a human support system, guiding and repatterning the healee's weakened and disrupted vital-energy flow to the end that the healee's own immunological system is stimulated and recovery is strengthened and reinforced.
>
> Working from a center of clarity is of prime importance, we can now recognize, because in responsibly intervening in another's life we must be aware of why, as well as how, we are intervening.[8]

The chakra-system comprising centres of energy (and consciousness) is acknowledged and worked with in therapeutic touch, as it is also in reiki and certainly by some spiritual healers.

> The heart chakra is the integrative center for the entire chakra system and, therefore, would be centrally involved in all states of illness or weakness of the physical body.[9]

To train as a therapeutic touch therapist means nothing less than the opportunity to acquire a new awareness and consciousness for the vital human energy field, and the ability to both sense and re-balance a person's field. This is a learning and experiencing process that changes the therapist and not only the patient. It is really an interaction that has the potential to heal the practitioner as well as the patient.

It is not possible to say more about reiki or therapeutic touch here, though it is clear that a thorough study of both these forms of healing would be important in terms of acquiring a better understanding and knowledge of their theory and practice. However it can be noted of both systems that unlike spiritual healing there is no mention of working co-operatively with guides and helpers in the spiritual world.

Each person must of course be free to choose his or her doctor, therapist, treatment, or healer, as circumstances permit. For those who are sick and suffering in body or mind, the primary need is to obtain the most effective help and support that can be offered, whatever its source may be. It is, however, precisely because it is often not so easy to determine what constitutes really effective healing help, that many people are looking at alternative and complementary approaches to healthcare. Clearly, in order to make the best informed choices, we must endeavour to learn more about and better understand what is on offer and how this may answer holistically the special needs of each individual, of you or me! Such healthy discrimination should therefore also be applied to the careful examination of the variety of hands-on healing which is available today.

Appendix 2
Further Extracts from Steiner

Rudolf Steiner makes some interesting references to psychic or spiritual healing in other lecture cycles, or single lectures, than those already quoted in the chapters of this book. I therefore include here the pertinent extracts from all the relevant lectures that I am at present aware of. Naturally it is recommended that, whenever possible, the lectures are also studied in their entirety.

In *Problems of Nutrition*:

> Weak as well as strong organisms can gain support from milk. If a person were to live exclusively on milk for a time, then not only would his regular forces be awakened but it would also go beyond this. He would receive from it an influx of forces giving him additional strength. A surplus of forces would be acquired that could be developed into healing forces. In order to possess a force, it must first be acquired, and in milk we see one means of developing certain forces in ourselves. Those who are moved by the earnestness of life to develop certain psychic healing forces, can train themselves to attain them. Naturally, we must remember that what is suitable for one, is not suitable for all. This is a matter for the individual. One person is able to do it, another not.[1]

In *The Spiritual Foundation of Morality*:

> It is, indeed, most striking and illuminating that in the case of a personality such as Francis of Assisi mighty moral impulses must have been active in order that he could perform his deeds. What sort of deeds were they? They were such that what they reveal is moral in the very highest sense of the word. Francis of Assisi was surrounded by people afflicted with very serious diseases for which the rest of the world at that time knew no cure. Moral impulses were so powerful in him that many lepers through him were given spiritual aid and great comfort. It is true that many could gain no more — but there were many others who by their faith and trust attained a stage where the moral impulses and forces which poured forth from Francis of Assisi had even a healing, health-giving effect.[2]

Steiner then asks the following question:

> What is the attitude which a man needs to hold regarding his fellow-man? It is that he needs the belief in the original goodness of humanity as a whole, and of each single human being in particular. That is the first thing we must say if we wish to speak at all in words concerning morality; that something immeasurably good lies at the bottom of human nature. That is what Francis of Assisi realised; and when he was approached by some of those stricken with the horrible disease we have described, as a good Christian of that day, he said somewhat as follows: 'A disease such as this is in a certain way the consequence of sin; but as sin is in the first instance spiritual error and disease the result, it must therefore be removed by a mighty opposing power.'

Hence Francis of Assisi saw by the sinner how, in a certain way, the punishment of sin manifests itself externally; but he also saw the good in human nature, he saw what lies at the bottom of each human being as divine spiritual forces. That which distinguished Francis of Assisi most was his sublime faith in the goodness lying in each human being, even in one who was being punished.

This made it possible for the contrary power to appear in his soul, and this is the power of love which gives and helps morally, and indeed even heals.[3]

In *The Gospel of St John and its Relation to the Other Gospels:*

You have already gathered from intimations in the last lectures that in older epochs — up to the time when the Christ impulse entered human evolution — the influence of soul upon soul was much stronger. Such was human disposition at that time. A man did not merely hear what was told him in externally audible words: in a certain way he could feel and know what the other felt and thought vividly, livingly. Love was something quite different from what it is today, albeit in those times it was largely a matter of blood ties. Nowadays it has taken on more of a psychic character, but it has lost its strength. Nor will it regain this until the Christ impulse shall have entered all human hearts. In olden times, active love possessed at the same time a healing property, a powerful balm, for the soul of its recipient.

Coincident with the development of the intellect and of cleverness, qualities that came into being only gradually, these ancient direct influences of soul upon soul dwindled away. The ability to act upon the other's soul, to cause one's own soul force to stream into it, was a gift possessed by ancient peoples. You must therefore imagine the force that one soul could receive from another as much greater, the influence one soul could exert upon another as much stronger, than is the case today. Although external historical documents report nothing of all this, and tablets and monuments do not mention it, clairvoyant study of the Akasha Chronicle nevertheless discloses the fact that in these ancient times the healing of the sick, for example, was extensively accomplished through a psychic influence passing from the one to the other. And the soul was capable of much else as well. Though today it sounds like a fairy tale, it is a fact that in those times a man's will, if he so desired and had specially trained himself for the purpose, had the power to act soothingly upon the growth of a plant, to accelerate or retard it. Today but scanty remnants of all this are left.

Human life, then, was very different at that time. No one would have been surprised — given the right mutual relationship — at the passing over of a psychic influence from one person to another. It must be kept in mind, however, that two or more were needed if the exercise of a psychic influence of that sort was to take effect. We could imagine the possibility of a man imbued with the power of Christ entering our midst nowadays; but those with the requisite faith in him would be very few in number, so that he would not be able to achieve all that can be accomplished by the influence of one soul upon another. For not only must the influence be exerted, someone must be present who is sufficiently developed to receive it. Remembering that formerly those who could receive such influences were more numerous, we should not be surprised to learn that for the healing of the sick there indeed existed the means by which psychic influences could take effect, but also, that influences which today can be transmitted only by mechanical means were at that time applied psychically.[4]

In *At the Gates of Spiritual Science:*

Higher self-knowledge begins only when we can say that our higher self is not in our ordinary 'I.' It is in the whole great world outside, in the sun and the moon, in a stone or an animal: everywhere can be found the same essential being that is in us. If a man says, 'I wish to cultivate my higher self and to withdraw from the world; I want to know nothing about anything material,' he entirely fails to understand that the higher self is everywhere outside, and that his own higher self is only a small part of the Great Self outside. Certain methods of so-called 'spiritual' healers make this mistake, which can be very serious. They instil into patients the idea that matter has no real existence and so there can be no illnesses. This notion is based on a false self-knowledge, and, as I have said, it can be dangerous. This healing method calls itself Christian, but in fact it is anti-Christian.[5]

What Steiner is referring to here is clearly not the 'spiritual healing' which is the subject of this book.

In *The Challenge of the Times*:

I must speak to you also regarding a third capacity, which is latent today but which will evolve. This is what I venture to call the hygienic occult capacity. Now we have all three: the materialistic occult capacity, the eugenic occult capacity, and the hygienic occult capacity. This hygienic occult capacity is well on its way and will not be long, relatively speaking, in arriving. This capacity will come to maturity simply through the insight that human life, in its course from birth to death, progresses in a manner identical with the process of an illness. Processes of illnesses are, in other words, only special and radical transmutations of the quite ordinary, normal life process taking its course between birth and death, except that we bear within ourselves not only the forces that create illness but also those that heal. These healing forces, as every occultist knows, are precisely the same as those that are applied when a person acquires occult capacities, in which case these forces are transmuted into the forces of knowledge. The healing power innate in the human organism, when transmuted into knowledge, gives occult forms of knowledge.

Now, every knowing person in the Western circles is aware that materialistic medicine will have no basis in the future. As soon as the hygienic occult capacities evolve, a person will need no external material medicine, but the possibility will exist of treating prophylactically in a psychic way to prevent those illnesses that do not arise through karmic causes because karmic illnesses cannot be influenced. Everything in this respect will change. This seems at present like a mere fantasy, but it is actually something that will soon come about. ... The potentiality of hygienic occult capacities is present in special measure among the people of the Central Countries [of Europe]. English-speaking people cannot acquire the hygienic occult capacities through their inborn potentialities, but they can acquire these capacities in their development in the course of time between birth and death. These can become acquired characteristics during that time. In the case of the population occupying the area approximately eastward from the Rhine and all the way into Asia, these capacities will be present on the basis of birth.[6]

Clearly what Steiner is predicting in this lecture are largely certain *inborn* capacities distributed on a geographic basis and in connection with definite potentials which will become available in the future evolution of humanity. Dr Michaela Glöckler also makes reference to this particular lecture by Steiner in her important book, *Medicine at the Threshold of a New Consciousness* (Temple Lodge, 1997).

However, the reality of spiritual healing as discussed in the present book, lays emphasis on the *conscious* development and training of healership in our modern time.

In *Between Death and Rebirth*:

I want now to speak of so-called spiritual healing. Here again it is not the movements or manipulations carried out by the healer that are of prime importance; they are necessary, but only as preparation. The aim is to establish a condition of rest, of balance. Whatever is outwardly visible in a case of spiritual healing is only the preparation for what the healer is trying to do; it is the final result that is of importance. In such a case the situation is like weighing something on a pair of scales: first, we put in the one scale what we want to weigh; in the other scale we put a weight and this sets the beam moving to right and left. But it is only when equilibrium has been established that we can read the weight. Something similar is true of actions in the spiritual worlds.[7]

Immediately prior to these interesting remarks on spiritual healing, Rudolf Steiner had been speaking about the great importance of acquiring a state of inner tranquillity and inner rest, both in order to receive revelations from the spiritual world and also to bring about something in the spiritual world. He says:

> Thus paradoxical as it may seem, our activity in the higher worlds depends upon our own inner tranquillity; the calmer we can become, the more will the facts of the spiritual world be able to come to expression through us.[8]

As the reader will recall, a healer needs to come to peace and quiet in him or herself in order to be an *attuned channel,* or instrument, for the healing energies to flow from the spiritual source to the recipient.

In *The Gospel of St Luke*:

> Thus we are shown quite clearly how the Christ-Ego worked upon all the other members of man's being. That is the essential point. The writer of the Gospel of St Luke, who gives special prominence in these parts of the Gospel to descriptions of the healings, wished to show how the healing influences proceeding from the Ego indicate the attainment of a lofty level in the evolutionary process; and he shows how Christ worked upon the astral body, the etheric body and the physical body of man. St Luke has set before us this great Ideal of evolution, 'Look towards your future! Your Ego, in the present stage of its development, is still weak; as yet it has little mastery. But it will gradually become master of the astral body, the etheric body and the physical body, and will transform them. Before you is set the great Ideal of Christ

> who reveals to mankind what this mastery can mean![9]

The whole of Lecture 8 is very relevant to understanding the nature and power of healing in earlier, ancient, epochs.

Perhaps until our own Egos have indeed progressed further on the path of evolution we are meantime greatly helped by the friends and guides on the other side of the threshold to give us the healing energies that are urgently required to help others?

The author would be very grateful to hear from anyone who knows of any further indications which Rudolf Steiner has given on psychic or spiritual healing. He can be contacted at the following address:

The Sheiling School
Camphill Community
Thornbury Park
Park Road
Thornbury
Bristol BS35 1HP

References

The Author

1 See Pietzner, 1990

Introduction

1 Brennan, 1988; Shine 1990; Hogan 2002
2 Shepherd, 1971
3 See Davy, 1975
4 See Evans & Rodger, 1992
5 Shepherd, 1971, p.194
6 Steiner, 1987, p.118

Chapter 1

1 UK Healers, 2003
2 Edwards, 1974, p.11
3 Edwards, 1974; 1993; 1998
4 Brennan 1988; 1993
5 Edwards, 1974, p.13
6 See Edwards 1993; 1998
7 Edwards, 1974, p.23
8 Bek & Pullar, 1986, p.113

Chapter 2

1 Steiner, 1994A
2 Steiner, 1951, p.296
3 See, for example, Steiner, 1973; 1976; 1978
4 Steiner, 1978, p.23
5 See Steiner, 1972
6 See Steiner, 1969A
7 Bek & Pullar, 1986, p.136
8 Evans & Rodger, 1992, p. 64
9 See Leroi, 1988
10 Steiner, 1997A, p.396

Chapter 3

1 See also Steiner, 1970B
2 Steiner, 1911B
3 Steiner, 1911B, see page 43
4 Steiner, 1911B, see page 43
5 John 15:7–12 *New English Bible*.
6 See Merry, 1963; Leroi, 1988; Steiner, 1975B
7 Steiner, 1969A, p.221
8 See Zajonc, 1993.
9 Steiner, 1969A, p.222
10 Steiner, 1969A, p.222
11 Steiner, 1969A, pp.226f
12 Steiner, 1969A, pp.230f
13 Steiner, 1969A, p.233

Chapter 4

1 Steiner, 1969A, p.225
2 Edwards, 1974, p.134
3 Edwards, 1974, p.135
4 Edwards, 1974, p.135
5 Steiner, 1997B, pp. 85f
6 Steiner, 1997B, pp. 86–88

Chapter 5

1 See Edwards, 1974, pp.31–34

Chapter 6

1 Latham, 2000, p.76
2 Steiner, 1979, p.13
3 Steiner, 1979, p.35
4 Edwards, 1974, p.89

5 Brennan, 1988; Shine, 1990
6 Steiner, 1994A
7 See Angelo, 1998; Bradford, 1999; Brennan, 1988
8 Lowndes, 1988, p.17
9 Bek & Pullar, 1986, p.107

Chapter 7

1 See Angelo, 1998
2 Edwards, 1974, p.88
3 Branch, 1982, p.111
4 Steiner, 1964, p.24
5 Steiner, 1964, p.29
6 Steiner, 1999, p.8
7 Steiner, 1975A, p.232
8 Leroi, 1988, p.49
9 See, for example, Williamson, 1996; Van Praagh, 1998; Shine, 1999.
10 Steiner, 1970A, p.34
11 see Wetzl, 1974
12 Steiner, 1969B, p.235
13 Bek & Pullar, 1986, p.77f

Conclusion

1 See Gerber, 2000.
2 Steiner, 1975B
3 Nesfield-Cookson, 1986, p.163 from Steiner, 1976, pp.224f
4 1 Cor.13. 4–7 *New English Bible*

Appendix 1

1 Gerber, 2000, p.402
2 Leir Shuffrey, 2000, p.3
3 Leir Shuffrey, 2000, p.70
4 See Way, 2000
5 Sandi Leir-Suffrey (2000)
6 Dolores Krieger's (1997)
7 Macrae, 1990, p.3
8 Krieger, 1997, p.17
9 Krieger, 1997, p.60

Appendix 2

1 *Problems of Nutrition*.GA68. Single lecture. 8 January 1909. The Anthroposophic Press, 1978 p.21
2 *The Spiritual Foundation of Morality*. GA155 Lecture 2. 29 May 1912. Steiner Book Centre Inc., Canada p.30
3 *Ibid* pp. 50–51
4 *The Gospel of St John and its relation to the other Gospels.* GA112. Lecture 9. 24 June to 7 July 1909. The Anthroposophic Press, 1982 pp.159-161
5 *At the Gates of Spiritual Science*. GA95 Lecture 14. 22 August to 4 September 1906. Rudolf Steiner Press, 1970 p.131
6 *The Challenge of the Times*. GA186 Lecture 3. 1 December 1918. The Anthroposophic Press, 1941 pp.97–99
7 *Between Death and Rebirth*. GA141 Lecture 1. 5 November 1912. Rudolf Steiner Press, 1975 p.23
8 *Ibid*, p. 22
9 *The Gospel of St Luke*. GA114 Lecture 8. 15 September to 26 September 1909. Rudolf Steiner Press, 1975, pp. 162f.

Selected Literature on Spiritual Healing

Angelo, Jack. *Your Healing Power*. Piatkus. 1998
This fully illustrated and comprehensive guide can be used as a self-healing manual, as a reference book for healers, and also as a workshop text. It is essential reading for all NFSH training courses. It is also a step-by-step practical course for those who wish to awaken and develop their own healing gift.

Angelo, Jack. *Spiritual Healing, a practical guide to Hands-On Healing*. A Godsfield Book. 2002.
Jack Angelo's latest book, it offers the first full-colour guide to spiritual healing.

Bek, Lilla & Pullar, Philippa. *The Seven Levels of Healing*. Rider. 1986.
This insightful and original book is said to represent a landmark in the history of the National Federation of Spiritual Healers. Unfortunately it is no longer in print but it may be possible to obtain a copy through the library service — as I did!

Bradford, Michael. *Hands-On Spiritual Healing*. Findhorn Press. 1999.
This book has been specifically designed as an easy-to-read training manual to demystify the art of healing, and to help readers awaken their own natural healing talents quickly and easily.

Branch, Ramus. *Harry Edwards, the life story of the great healer*. 1982.
A comprehensive and fascinating biography of the great healer, written by his close friend and associate healer. From Harry Edwards' birth to his final hours, the story of his long life is told with a rare insight into his remarkable and complex character.

Brennan, Barbara. *Hands of Light*. Bantam Books. 1988.
This guide to healing through the human energy field is written by a practising healer, psychotherapist, and scientist. She also has her own School of Healing. There are many colour illustrations in this rather technical but impressive volume. Brennan's second book published in 1993 is entitled, *Light Emerging*.

Butler, Patrick. *Develop your power to heal*. Quantum. 2002.
A practical development course in healing, with exercises and assessments designed to develop your powers and demonstrate your progress. Contains also some humourous incidents from his own healing practice, and also incorporates the 'Code of Conduct' of the Confederation of Healing Organizations.

Edwards, Harry.* *A Guide to the understanding and practice of Spiritual Healing*. 1974.
In this comprehensive volume Edwards draws upon his vast healing experience to explain how spiritual healing is accomplished. Important both for the beginner and for those who are already accomplished healers. The book continues to be regularly revised and updated.

Edwards, Harry. *Spirit Healing*. 1993.
Informative and clearly written and first published in 1960, it is still a source of guidance and insight for healers.

Edwards, Harry. *The Power of Spiritual Healing*. 1998.
Illustrating his points with case histories Edwards shows that the healing purpose, apart from the healing of the sick, is also to prevent disease in the future and to awaken man's spiritual consciousness.

Fare, Dennis. *Spiritual Healing — some interesting case histories*. Dennis Fare Healing Centre, 33 The Park, Kingswood, Bristol BS15 4BL.

* All Harry Edwards books can be obtained from: The Healer Publishing Co Ltd. Burrows Lea, Shere, Guildford, Surrey GU5 9QG

Selected Literature on Spiritual Healing

A small privately printed booklet written by an outstanding healer. Exemplifies his great dedication and patience. Some copies are still available upon request.

Hogan, Tony. *Born to Heal*. Rider. 2002.
This is the autobiography of a man who has devoted his life to restoring health and happiness to all those who come to him. He is one of Ireland's leading spiritual healers. A video documentary of his life and work is also available.

Markides, Kyriacos C. *The Magus of Strovolus — the extraordinary world of a spiritual healer*. Penguin Books. 1990.
The trilogy of books by Kyriacos C Markides, the first of which is *The Magus of Strovolus* could be of especial interest to students of anthroposophy, since in these books Markides describes his experiences with a spiritual healer who was also an Initiate. This initiate referred to as 'Daskalos' by Markides, was identified by Richard Leviton (1994) in his book *The Imagination of Pentecost* as Stylianos Atteshlis, the Cypriot magus and Researcher of Truth.

Shine, Betty. *Mind to Mind*. Corgi Books. 1990.
Betty Shine's extraordinary gifts — a clairvoyant power to diagnose medically, her healing and mediumistic powers and her discovery of 'mind energy' — have made her one of Britain's foremost healers. Contains many fascinating case histories. She died in April 2002.

White, Ruth *Energy Healing for Beginners — a step by step guide to the basics of spiritual healing*. Piatkus. 2002.
A step-by-step guide to the basics of spiritual healing. Ruth White is also a transpersonal psychotherapist and spiritual teacher who runs workshops throughout Britain and other parts of Europe. She has written numerous books.

Bibliography

Angelo, J. 1998. *Your Healing Power*. Piatkus.

BAHA. 2002. *Training Guide for Tutors and Probationers*.

Bek, L. & Pullar, P. 1986. *The Seven Levels of Healing*. Rider.

Bradford, M. 1999. *Hands-on Spiritual Healing*. Findhorn Press.

Branch, R. 1982. *Harry Edwards — the life story of the great healer.* The Healer Publishing Co Ltd.

Brennan, B. 1988. *Hands of Light*. Bantam Books.

—, 1993. Light Emerging. Bantam Books.

Davy, J. 1975. *Work Arising from the life of Rudolf Steiner*. Rudolf Steiner Press, London.

Edwards, H. 1974. *A Guide to the understanding and practice of Spiritual Healing*. The Healer Publishing Co Ltd.

—, 1993. *Spirit Healing*. The Healer Publishing Co Ltd.

—, 1998. *The Power of Spiritual Healing*. The Healer Publishing Co Ltd.

Evans, M. & Rodger, I. 1992. *Anthroposophical Medicine*. Thorsons, London.

Fuller, J G. 1975. *Arigo — Surgeon of the rusty knife*. Hart-Davis, MacGibbon, London.

Gerber, R. 2000. *Vibrational Medicine for the 21st Century*. Piatkus.

Hogan, T. 2002. *Born to Heal*. Rider.

House of Lords. Science and Technology — Sixth Report. *Complementary and Alternative Medicine*. 21 November 2000.

Krieger, D. 1997. *Therapeutic Touch Inner Workbook*. Bear & Company Inc.

Latham, C. 2000. *The Heart of Healing*. Findhorn Press.

Leroi, R. 1988. *Illness and Healing in the context of Cosmic Evolution*. Temple Lodge

Lowndes, F. 1998. *Enlivening the Chakra of the Heart*. Sophia Books, Rudolf Steiner Press, London.

Macrae, J. 1990. *Therapeutic Touch a practical guide*. Arkana.

Merry, E. 1963. *The Ascent of Man*. New Knowledge Books.

Nesfield-Cookson, B. 1983. *Rudolf Steiner's Vision of Love*. The Aquarian Press.

Pietzner, C., ed. 1990. *A Candle on the Hill, images of Camphill life*. Floris Books.

Quest, P. 2002. *Reiki for Life*. Piatkus.

Shepherd, A.P. 1971. *A Scientist of the Invisible.* Hodder & Stoughton, London.

Shine, B. 1990. *Mind to Mind*. Corgi Books.

—, 1991. *Mind Magic — the key to the universe.* Corgi Books.

—, 1999. *My Life as a Medium*. Harper Collins.

Shuffrey, S.L. 2000. *Reiki*. Teach Yourself Books.

Solomon, G. 1997. *Stephen Turoff — Psychic Surgeon*. Thorsons.

Steiner, R. 1906, 1970. *At the Gates of Spiritual Science.* Rudolf Steiner Press. London. (Complete Works (GA) No. 95)

—, 1907, 1981. *Theosophy of the Rosicrucian.* Rudolf Steiner Press. London. (GA 99).

—, 1911A, 1964. *Faith, Love, Hope*. Steiner Book Centre, Canada. (GA 130).

—, 1911B. *The Work of the Ego in Childhood*. Anthroposophical Quarterly, Vol. 21, No. 4, Winter 1976. (GA 127).

—, 1951. *The Course of my Life.* Anthroposophic Press. New York. (GA 28).

—, 1964. *The Dead are with us*. Rudolf Steiner Press, London. (GA 182)

—, 1969A. *The Manifestations of Karma*. Rudolf Steiner Press, London. (GA 120).

—, 1969B. *True and False Paths in Spiritual Investigation*. Rudolf Steiner Press, London. (GA 243).

—, 1970A. *At the Gates of Spiritual Science*. Rudolf Steiner Press, London. (GA 95).

—, 1970B. *The Spiritual Guidance of Man and Humanity.* Anthroposophic Press, New York.

—, 1972. *Christ and the Human Soul*. Rudolf Steiner Press, London. (GA 155).

—, 1973. *From Jesus to Christ*. Rudolf Steiner Press, London. (GA 131).

—, 1975A. *Life between death and rebirth*. Anthroposophic Press, New York. (GA 140).

—, 1975B. *The Gospel of St. Luke.* Rudolf Steiner Press, London.

—, 1976. *The Christ Impulse and the development of ego consciousness.* Anthroposophic Press, New York. (GA 116).

—, 1978. *The Fifth Gospel*. Rudolf Steiner Press, London. (GA 148).

—, 1979. *The Bridge between Universal Spirituality and the Physical Constitution of Man*. Anthroposophic Press, New York. (GA 202).

—, 1987. *Pastoral Medicine.* Anthroposophic Press, New York.

—, 1994A. *How to know Higher Worlds*. Anthroposophic Press. New York. (GA 10).

—, 1994B. *Theosophy — an introduction to the spiritual processes in human life and in the cosmos*. Anthroposophic Press, New York. (GA 9).

—, 1997A. *An Outline of Esoteric Science*. Anthroposophic Press, New York. (GA 13).

—, 1997B. *Course for Young Doctors*. Mercury Press, New York. (GA 316).

—, 1999. Ed. Bamford, C. *Staying Connected*. Anthroposophic Press, New York.

The Alliance Review. No.41. December 1999.

The Alliance Review. No.43. December 2000.

The New English Bible. 1970. *The New Testament*. Oxford U.P. Cambridge U.P.

UK HEALERS. 2003. Standards. Version 3.5. November 2003.

Van Praagh, J. 1998. *Talking to Heaven — a medium's message of life after death*. BCA.

Way, B. 2000. *Healing Energies, understanding and using hands-on healing*. Simon & Schuster, Australia.

Wetzl, J. 1974. *The Bridge over the River*. Anthroposophic Press, New York.

Williamson, L. 1996. *Contacting the Spirit World*. Piatkus.

WFH. 2003. *Training Manual*.

Woodward, B. & Hogenboom, M. 2002. *Autism — A Holistic Approach*. Floris Books.

Zajonc, A. 1993. *Catching the Light*. Oxford University Press.

Useful Addresses

The General Anthropposophical Society
The Goetheanum
CH-4143 Dornach
Switzerland
Email:
sekretariat@goetheanum.ch
www.goetheanum.ch

Anthroposophical Society in Great Britain
Rudolf Steiner House
35 Park Road
London NW1 6XT
Tel: 0207 723 4400
('Rudolf Steiner Press' and 'The Library' are at the same address)

World Federation of Healing
Secretary General
1 The Oaks
Hexham
Northumberland NE46 2PZ
Email: alexa.dymond@btopen-world.com

British Alliance of Healing Associations (BAHA)
Ken Baker (Chairman)
7 Ashcombe Drive
Edenbridge
Kent TN8 6JY
www.bahahealing.co.uk

U.K. Healers
PO Box 4137
London W1A 6F
Email: admin@ukhealers.info
www.ukhealers.info

National Federation of Spiritual Healers (NFSH)
Old Manor Farm Studio
Church Street
Sunbury-on-Thames
Middlesex TW16 6RG
Email: office@nfsh.org.uk
www.nfsh.org.uk

The Harry Edwards Spiritual Healing Sanctuary
Burrows Lea
Hook Lane
Shere, Guildford
Surrey GU5 9QG
Email: info@burrowslea.org.uk
www.harryedwards.org.uk

Confederation of Healing Organizations (CHO)
Tony Ashenden
250 Chicherter Road
Portsea, Portsmouth PO1 3HB
Tel: 02392 693169

European Confederation of Healing Organizations (ECHO)
Rev. Michael Baker
Bleich Str. 40
D33102 Paderborn, Germany
Email: michael.baker@online.de

Spiritualists National Union (SNU)
Minister Chris Denton
36 Newmarket, Otley
W. Yorks LS21 3AE
Email:
healing@cpdenton.freeserve.co.uk

Index